New American STREAMLINE

BERNARD HARTLEY & PETER VINEY

DESTINATIONS

An intensive American English series for advanced students
Student Book

REVISED BY IRENE FRANKEL
with contributions by PETER VINEY

Oxford University Press

Oxford University Press

198 Madison Avenue
New York, NY 10016 USA

Walton Street
Oxford OX2 6DP England

OXFORD is a trademark of Oxford University Press

Library of Congress Cataloging-in-Publication Data
Hartley, Bernard.
    Destinations: an intensive American English series
for advanced students: student book / Bernard Hartley
& Peter Viney; revised by Irene Frankel and Peter
Viney.
        p.   cm. -- (New American streamline)
    "Third book in the [unnumbered] series"--CIP info.
    ISBN 0-19-434833-4 (student bk.).--ISBN 0-19-434835-
0 (teacher bk.).--ISBN 0-19-434836-9 (cassette).--ISBN 0-
19-434849-0 (CD)
    1. English language--Textbooks for foreign speakers.
I. Viney, Peter. II. Frankel, Irene. III. Title. IV. Series:
Hartley, Bernard. New American streamline.
PE1128.H3756 1995
428.2'4--dc20   95-3687

Printing (last digit) 10 9 8 7 6 5 4 3 2

Printed in Hong Kong

Based on the American adaptation by Flamm/Northam
Authors and Publishers Services, Inc.

Editorial Manager: Susan Lanzano
Editor: Ken Mencz
Senior Designer: Sharon Hudak
Art Buyer: Tracy Hammond
Picture Researcher: Paul Hahn
Production Manager: Abram Hall

Cover illustration by: Pete Kelly

Illustrations and realia by: Eliot Bergman, Claudia
Kehrhahn, Frank Magadan, Karen Minot, Tom
Newsom, Tom Powers, Paul Sample, Max Seabaugh,
Terri Starrett, Darren Thompson, Tudor Art Studios
Ltd., Turnround Studio, Rose Zgodzinski

Location and studio photography by: Peter Chin, Milton
Heiberg, Dennis Kitchen

*The publishers would like to thank the following for their
permission to reproduce photographs*: Evan Agostini/
Liaison International, Jeff Amberg/Liaison
International, Sandra Baker/Liaison International,
Peter Beck/The Stock Market, Bettman Archive, J.
Chenet/Liaison International, Gary Chowanetz/
The Stock Market, Tobias Everke/Liaison International,
John Feingersh/The Stock Market, Frank Fisher/
Liaison International, Pam Francis/Liaison
International, Ken Frick/International Stock, Globe
Photos, Charles Gupton/The Stock Market, Halebian/
Liaison International, Dirck Halstead/Liaison
International, Niklas Hill/Liaison International, Chip
Hires/Liaison International, Hulton-Deutch Library,
Mark Kelly, Barry King/Liaison International,
Barbara Kirk/The Stock Market, B. Kluckhohn/Liaison
International, Nick Koudis/The Stock Market, Allen
Levenson/Tony Stone Images, Liaison International,
Andy Lyons/Allsport, John Maher/The Stock Market,
Roy Morsch/The Stock Market, Mugshots/The Stock
Market, Nancy Ney/The Stock Market, Peter Newark's
Western Americana, Kunio Owaki/The Stock Market,
Bryan Peterson/The Stock Market, Photofest, David
Pollack/The Stock Market, Germain Rey/Liaison
International, Chris Rogers/The Stock Market, Sam
Sargent/Liaison International, Bob Schatz/Liaison
International, Roy Schneider/The Stock Market, John
Schreiber/The Stock Market, Chris Schwarz, Schwenke/
Courtesy, Cohn and Wolfe, Robert Slack/International
Stock, F. Spooner/Liaison International, Jan Staller/
The Stock Market, The Stock Market, Swanson/Liaison
International, Steve Swope/Allsport, William Taufic/
The Stock Market, WCS Thompson/The Stock Market,
Times Newspapers Ltd., Tom Tracy/The Stock Market,
Terry Williams

(If notified, the publisher will be pleased to rectify any
errors or omissions at the earliest opportunity.)

The publishers would like to thank the following companies:
MasterCard International, McDonald's Corporation,
Nissin Foods (USA) Co., Inc., Washington Metropolitan
Area Transit Authority

Students can buy a cassette or CD which
contains a recording of the texts and dialogues in this book.

A: Excuse me. Dolores Cotten?

B: Yes?

A: Hi. I'm Brad Jordan...from Lemon Computers? How do you do?

B: How do you do? I'm glad to meet you, Brad. Thank you for coming to meet us.

A: It's a pleasure. How was the trip?

B: Fine. Oh, I'd like you to meet Ron Eng. He's our sales manager.

A: How do you do, Ron?

Exercise 1

A: Bob Crawford?

B: . . .?

A: Hello. I'm Helen Kirby, from General Technologies. How do you do?

B: . . . .

A: It's a pleasure. Did you have a good trip?

B: . . . .

A: Oh, let me introduce you to Charlie Vitto. He's our financial manager.

B: . . . .

C: Karen!

D: Hi, Jody. How are you doing?

C: Great. How are you? I haven't seen you for ages.

D: I'm all right. Are you here to meet somebody?

C: No, my mom just left for Miami.

D: Do you have time for coffee?

C: Sure. I'd love some.

E: Margaret, hi.

F: Hello, Carol. How are you?

E: Oh, I'm OK. How are you getting along?

F: Fine, thanks. How are Larry and the kids?

E: Everybody's fine. My car's just outside. Let me take one of your bags.

F: Oh, thanks. Careful, it's heavy.

Gate 4

G: Hi. What time is your next flight to New York?

H: Two forty-five. Flight 604 to La Guardia Airport. There's space available.

G: What's the one-way fare?

H: It's $228.70 with tax.

G: OK. There you go. Put it on my Visa card, please.

H: All right. Just a second.

Exercise 2

Look at the conversation between **G** and **H,** and practice two similar conversations, one for Boston and one for Chicago.

Air Streamline Departures from Middleburg		
Service to	Flight	Departs
Boston (Logan)	317	11:05AM
New York (La Guardia)	604	2:45PM
Los Angeles (LAX)	410	4:15PM
Chicago (O'Hare)	104	3:55PM
Atlanta	211	10:20PM

Air Streamline Fares (tax included)

Fares			
From	Middleburg		
To	Boston	*one-way*	$228.70
		round-trip	$457.40
To	Chicago	*one-way*	$128.20
		round-trip	$256.40

I: Well, hi there!

J: Uh—hello.

I: How are you doing?

J: Oh—fine. Uh—excuse me.... Do I know you from somewhere?

I: Sure, it's me, Rick Ballestrina.

J: I'm sorry. I don't think I know you.

I: Aren't you José Cortes?

J: No, I'm afraid not.

I: Oh, excuse me. I thought you were someone else. I'm so sorry.

J: That's all right.

🎧 Listening

Listen to the airport announcements. Look at the example and complete the chart in the same way.

Airline	Flight	To	Gate	Departs
1. Air Streamline	604	New York (JFK)	3	2:45
2.				
3.				
4.				
5.				

Exercise 3

How are you?
I'm fine, thanks. How are you?

1. Hi!
2. I'm so sorry.
3. Thank you very much for coming to meet us.
4. Aren't you Michael Jackman?
5. How are you getting along?
6. There you go.
7. Excuse me.
8. Good-bye.

Is everything ready?

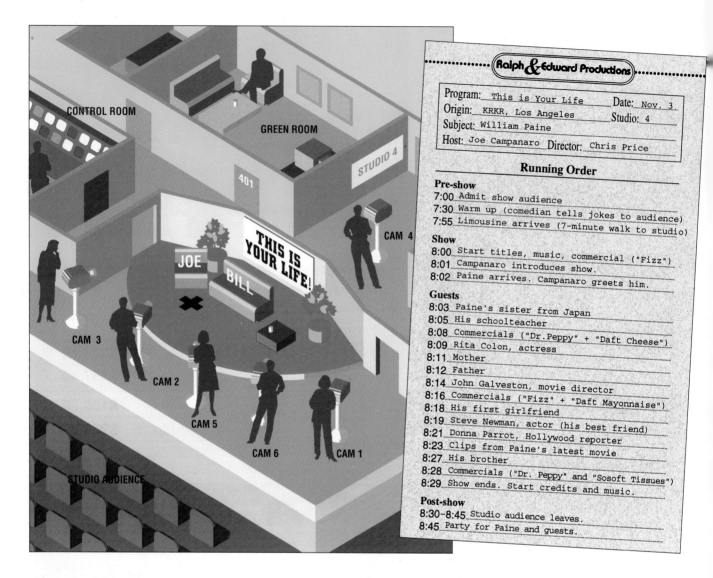

Ralph & Edward Productions

Program: This is Your Life   Date: Nov. 3
Origin: KRKR, Los Angeles   Studio: 4
Subject: William Paine
Host: Joe Campanaro Director: Chris Price

Running Order

Pre-show
7:00 Admit show audience
7:30 Warm up (comedian tells jokes to audience)
7:55 Limousine arrives (7-minute walk to studio)

Show
8:00 Start titles, music, commercial ("Fizz")
8:01 Campanaro introduces show
8:02 Paine arrives. Campanaro greets him.

Guests
8:03 Paine's sister from Japan
8:05 His schoolteacher
8:08 Commercials ("Dr.Peppy" + "Daft Cheese")
8:09 Rita Colon, actress
8:11 Mother
8:12 Father
8:14 John Galveston, movie director
8:16 Commercials ("Fizz" + "Daft Mayonnaise")
8:18 His first girlfriend
8:19 Steve Newman, actor (his best friend)
8:21 Donna Parrot, Hollywood reporter
8:23 Clips from Paine's latest movie
8:27 His brother
8:28 Commercials ("Dr. Peppy" and "Sosoft Tissues")
8:29 Show ends. Start credits and music.

Post-show
8:30-8:45 Studio audience leaves.
8:45 Party for Paine and guests.

This Is Your Life is a very popular show on American TV. Every week, they invite a well-known person to a TV studio. The person doesn't know that he or she will be the subject of the program. The host greets the person with "This Is Your Life!" The person then meets friends and relatives from the past and present. They tape the program before a live audience. The taping begins at eight o'clock. It's 6:45 now and the director is checking the preparations with her new production assistant. The subject of tonight's show will be an actor, William Paine. The host, as usual, will be Joe Campanaro.

Director: OK. We're bringing Bill Paine here in a rented limousine. He thinks he's coming to tape a talk-show appearance. We've told the driver to arrive at exactly 7:55. The program begins at eight o'clock. At that time, Bill will be walking to the studio. Joe will start

his introduction at 8:01, and Bill will get here at 8:02. Joe will meet him at the door. Camera 4 will be there. Then he'll take him to that sofa. It'll be on Camera 3. Bill will be sitting there during the whole program. For most of the show, Joe will be sitting next to the sofa or standing on that "X." He'll be on Camera 2. The guests will come through that door, talk to Bill and Joe, and then go backstage. Now, is that clear?

Production Assistant: Yes, but—uh—there is one thing…

Director: Well, what is it?

PA: Where will the guests be waiting before they come on?

Director: The green room—401. Stephanie will be sitting there with them. They'll be watching the show on a monitor. She'll cue them two minutes before they come on.

PA: OK. I think that covers everything.

Exercise 1

Each of the guests will say a few words about William Paine. Look at the running order above.
A: Who'll be speaking at 8:06?
B: His schoolteacher will.

Ask and answer about: 8:04, 8:10, 8:15, 8:19, and 8:27.

Exercise 2

A: What'll be happening at 7:45?
B: A comedian will be telling jokes to the audience.

Ask and answer about: 7:57, 8:35, and 9:00.

Exercise 3

The guests will be waiting in Room 401 from 7:50 until they go on.
A: How long will his sister be waiting?
B: She'll be waiting for 13 minutes.

Ask and answer about the other guests.

This Is Your Life!

Campanaro: Good evening and welcome to *This Is Your Life!* I'm your host, Joe Campanaro. We're waiting for the subject of tonight's program. He's one of the world's leading actors, and he thinks he's coming here for a talk show. I think I hear him now…. Yes, here he is! William Paine, this is your life!

Paine: Oh, no! I can't believe it! Not me….

Campanaro: Yes, you! Come in with me now. Ladies and gentlemen, William Paine! Sit right over here, Bill. Let's begin at the beginning. You were born in Providence, Rhode Island, on July 2, 1958. You were the youngest of six children. Your mother was a model, and your father worked at a furniture store. Of course, your name was Herman Wartski then.

Campanaro: Do you recognize this voice?

Voice: I remember Herm—uh, Bill—when he was two. He used to cry and scream all day.

Paine: Roseanne!

Campanaro: All the way from Tokyo—we flew her here to be with you tonight—your sister, Roseanne Wartski Tatsukawa.

Paine: Rosie, why didn't you tell me?

Campanaro: Yes, you haven't seen each other for nine years. Take a seat next to him, Roseanne. You went to school in Providence and got your diploma from Whitney High School in 1976.

Campanaro: Do you remember this voice?

Voice: Herman! Stop daydreaming! I asked you a question!

Paine: Incredible! It's Mr. Theissen.

Campanaro: Your English teacher, Mr. Irwin Theissen. Was Bill a good student, Mr. Theissen?

Theissen: Well, not really. No, he was the worst in the class. But he was a great actor, even in those days. He could imitate all the teachers.

Campanaro: Thank you, Mr. Theissen. You can talk to Bill later. Well, Bill, you went on to the Yale School of Drama in 1978 and finished in 1982. In 1983, you went to Hollywood.

Campanaro: Do you know this voice?

Voice: Say, Bill, can you ride a horse yet?

Paine: Rita!

Campanaro: Yes, Rita Colon, who's flown in from New York, where she's appearing in the new musical *The Romance Dance.*

Colon: Bill, darling! It's so wonderful to see you. Hello, Joe, darling. Bill and I were in a movie together in 1984. Bill had to learn to ride a horse, and…well, Bill doesn't like horses very much.

Paine: Like them? I'm scared to death of them!

Colon: Anyway, poor Bill practiced for two weeks. Then he went to the director—it was John Galveston—and said, "What do you want me to do?" John said, "I want you to fall off the horse." Bill was furious. He said, "What?! Fall off! I've been practicing for two weeks. I could fall off the first day—without any practice!"

Look at this:

Ralph & Edward Productions

Program: This is Your Life — Date: Nov. 3
Origin: KRKR, Los Angeles — Studio: 4
Subject: William Paine
Host: Joe Campanaro — Director: Chris Price

Subject's Biographical Data

Last name: Wartski (stage name: William Paine)

First Name: Herman

Middle name/initial: I

Date of birth: 7/2/58

Place of birth: Providence, RI

Nationality: American (U.S.)

Education: Whitney H.S. - Providence
Yale School of Drama, New Haven

Address: 77 Sunshine Boulevard
Hollywood, CA 90214

Marital status: Single

Occupation: Actor

Exercise

Ask another student questions and fill out the form.

Ralph & Edward Productions

Program: _____ Date: _____
Origin: _____ Studio: _____
Subject: _____
Host: _____ Director: _____

Subject's Biographical Data

Last name: _____

First Name: _____

Middle name/initial: _____

Date of birth: _____

Place of birth: _____

Nationality: _____

Education: _____

Address: _____

Marital status: _____

Occupation: _____

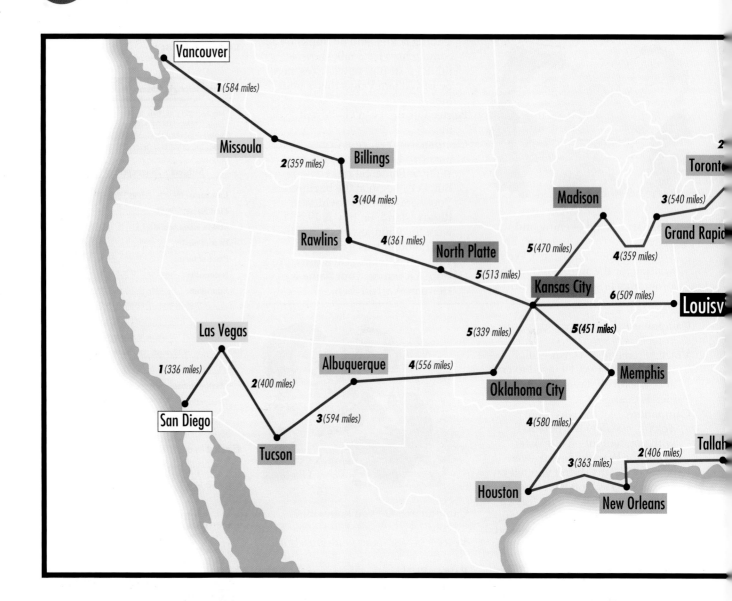

Vancouver

1 (584 miles)

Missoula

2 (359 miles)

Billings

3 (404 miles)

Rawlins

4 (361 miles)

North Platte

5 (513 miles)

Toronto

3 (540 miles)

Madison

Grand Rapid

5 (470 miles)

4 (359 miles)

Kansas City

6 (509 miles)

Louisv

5 (339 miles)

5 (451 miles)

Las Vegas

1 (336 miles)

Albuquerque

4 (556 miles)

Memphis

2 (400 miles)

San Diego

3 (594 miles)

Oklahoma City

4 (580 miles)

Tucson

Tallah

2 (406 miles)

3 (363 miles)

Houston

New Orleans

Driver: Eric Rogers
Region: Pacific Northwest
Age: 28
Starting point: Vancouver
Car: Pontiac Grand Am
Engine displacement: 2.3 l/140 cu in
Top speed: (estimate)108 mph
    (173 km/h)
Fuel economy: city 22 mpg, highway
    34 mpg
Overall dimensions
    Length: 187.9 in (477.3 cm)
    Width: 67.5 in (171.5 cm)
    Height: 53.4 in (135.6 cm)

Driver: Craig Halpern
Region: Southern California
Age: 32
Starting point: San Diego
Car: Chevrolet Lumina
Engine displacement: 3.4 l/207 cu in
Top speed: 135 mph (216 km/h)
Fuel economy: city 17 mpg, highway
    26 mpg
Overall dimensions
    Length: 198.3 in (503.7 cm)
    Width: 71.7 in (182.1 cm)
    Height: 53.4 in (135.6 cm)

Driver: Bernard Westbrook
Region: Southeast
Age: 31
Starting point: Miami
Car: Ford Thunderbird
Engine displacement: 3.8 l/231.3 cu in
Top speed: (estimate)145 mph
    (232 km/h)
Fuel economy: city 17 mpg, highway
    26 mpg
Overall dimensions
    Length: 200.7 in (509.8 cm)
    Width: 72.5 in (184.2 cm)
    Height: 53.6 in (136.1 cm)

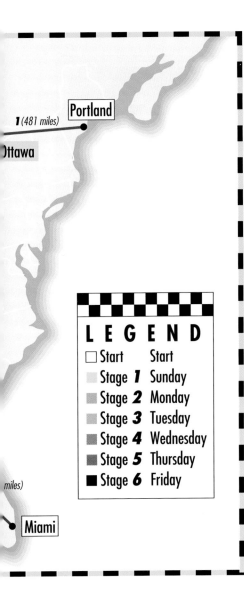

1 (481 miles)

Portland

Ottawa

LEGEND

☐ Start — Start
Stage **1** Sunday
Stage **2** Monday
Stage **3** Tuesday
Stage **4** Wednesday
Stage **5** Thursday
Stage **6** Friday

miles)

Miami

Driver: Alex Rossi
Region: Northeast
Age: 30
Starting point: Portland, Maine
Car: Chevrolet Monte Carlo
Engine displacement: 3.4 l/207 cu in
Top speed: (estimate)133 mph
(213 km/h)
Fuel economy: city 17 mpg, highway
23 mpg
Overall dimensions
Length: 200.3 in (508.8 cm)
Width: 72.7 in (184.7 cm)
Height: 52.5 in (133.4 cm)

The Louisville Rally, which started in 1991, is quickly becoming one of the most famous car events in the United States. Competitors leave from several points around North America and follow routes of approximately equal length to a rallying point, which will be Kansas City this year. Then they follow a single route to the finish. The rally consists of six daily stages, beginning on Sunday morning, and each competitor will have driven over 2,000 miles by Friday night. It is not a race. The winner is decided on a points system. Drivers have to maintain an average speed between control points, and there are also special tests of driving skill in different conditions on the way.

Exercise 1

Look at the information about the first driver.
What's his name?
His name's Eric Rogers.
What region does he represent?
He represents the Pacific Northwest.
How old is he?
He's 28.

Ask and answer questions about the other drivers.

Exercise 2

Look at the information about the first car.
What make is it?
It's a Pontiac Grand Am.
How fast can it go?
The top speed is 108 mph (173 km/h).
How much gas does it use?
22 mpg in the city, 34 mpg on the highway.
How long is it?
It's 187.9 in/477.3 cm.
How wide is it?
It's 67.5 in/171.5 cm.
How high is it?
It's 53.4 in/135.6 cm.

Ask and answer questions about the other cars.

Exercise 3

Look at the information about the drivers.
Bernard Westbrook's older than Alex Rossi.
Eric Rogers isn't as old as Bernard Westbrook.
Craig Halpern's the oldest.

Make comparisons about the cars using: fast/long/wide/high/economical.

Rally News from CSN, Cable Sports Network

Now here's a report from Bob Costello.

Bob: Hello from Billings, Montana. It's nine o'clock on Monday night, September 25, and the Pacific Northwest competitors in the Louisville Rally have just arrived here at the end of the second stage in this year's contest. Eric Rogers, who's driving a Pontiac Grand Am, is in the lead. Chris Sullivan, who won last year's rally, crashed near Spokane, Washington, this morning. Chris was not hurt, but he will be unable to continue. Seven other drivers have withdrawn due to bad weather conditions. Tonight the drivers, who left from Seattle on Sunday morning, will be heading into Wyoming.

Exercise 4

Look at Bob Costello's report and the map.
All the cars started on Sunday morning.
Where is the first driver now? He's in Billings, Montana.
Where did he start? He started in Vancouver.
How long has he been driving? He's been driving for two days.
How many miles has he driven? He's driven 584 miles (940 km).

Ask and answer questions about the other drivers.

Exercise 5

Look at the map. It's Monday night.
Where will Eric Rogers be tomorrow night? He'll be in Rawlins, Wyoming.
What will he be doing tomorrow? He'll be driving from Billings to Rawlins.

Ask and answer questions about Wednesday and Thursday.

Do the same for the other drivers.

Exercise 6

Look at the information about Eric Rogers.
On Tuesday night he'll be in Rawlins, Wyoming.
How far will he have driven on Tuesday?
He'll have driven 1,347 miles (2,167 km).

Ask and answer questions about Wednesday and Thursday.

Do the same for the other drivers.

The Romance Connection

Announcer: Welcome to *The Romance Connection*, where old-fashioned romance meets modern technology. Now here's your host, Joel Preiss.

Joel: Good evening, ladies and gentlemen. Our first guest tonight is Roxanne Matthews. Roxanne is a financial analyst. She likes skiing, snorkeling, and eating in good restaurants. Roxanne has been to all the four-star restaurants in the area! She loves going to the theater and the movies. She dates about once every two weeks, but she's tired of dating men who won't make a *Promise* commitment. Hello, Roxanne!

Roxanne: Hi, Joel. It's nice to be here.

Joel: Now let's see the tapes that Roxanne saw. And then you'll get a chance to vote on who she should go out with. First there was Mike.

Mike: Hi, Roxanne. Let me tell you a little about myself. I really enjoy cooking, and I'd love to have someone to cook for! I started painting a few months ago…watercolors of sunsets at the beach…and I'm really pretty good, if I must say so myself. I like playing tennis, going skiing, and going hiking. I'm quite an athlete, really. I'm not interested in rock climbing or skydiving…I'm scared of falling! But I don't mind falling in love.

Joel: Well, Mike sounds like quite a romantic. Next there was George.

George: Good evening, Roxanne. I enjoy getting dressed up and going out on the town…dinner in fine restaurants, the theater or concerts, dancing. I'm always trying new places…I get bored going to the same restaurants all the time. I also like driving fast cars and listening to my favorite CDs while I drive. I'd love having someone in the passenger seat sharing the experience with me.

Joel: Well, what do you think of that, Roxanne? And finally, there was Tim.

Tim: Hi, Roxanne. I love traveling to faraway places and seeing new sights. I've recently come back from a trip to the pyramids in Egypt. They're amazing. They make you believe that anything's possible. Now I'm interested in learning more about the ancient Egyptians. I enjoy eating great ethnic food and meeting people from other cultures. I gave up traveling with other people because no one I knew had my sense of adventure…but I'm not giving up looking for someone!

Joel: Well, there you have the three candidates for Roxanne. Now, audience, which one do you think Roxanne should go out with: Mike, George, or Tim?

Exercise 1

Discuss: Who should Roxanne go out with? Why?

Exercise 2

I like playing tennis.

Write sentences about yourself with: love/enjoy/like/don't like/dislike/hate/can't stand.

Exercise 3

I'm scared of falling.

Write sentences about yourself with: afraid of/terrified of/scared of.

Exercise 4

I get bored going to the same restaurants all the time.

Write sentences about yourself with: fed up with/bored with/tired of/interested in.

Exercise 5

I gave up traveling with other people.

Write sentences about yourself with: start/begin/stop/give up.

For some jobs, you have to fill out an application, usually in person. For other jobs, you have to send a résumé, which you include with a cover letter. After the employer looks over your application or résumé, you may be called for an interview. Here is part of a brochure which was put out by a state employment office. The office helps people who are looking for jobs.

THE INTERVIEW

What do I do well?	School activities?
What are my good points?	School subjects?
Why would I like this job?	Previous job?
Hobbies? Interests?	Part-time work?
What do I like doing and why?	
What do I not like doing and why?	

You will want to ask questions too:

The job itself?	Can I see where I would be working?
Training?	Hours?
Prospects for advancement?	Money?
Educational opportunities?	Conditions?

Write down your answers and go over them just before you go into the interview.

BEFORE THE INTERVIEW

1. Find out all you can about the company.
2. Find out the interviewer's name and office phone number.
3. Find out where the interview is.
4. Find out how to get there and how long it will take you to get there.
5. Make sure you know what the job involves.
6. Dress to look clean and neat.

AT THE INTERVIEW

DOs
1. Arrive early. Call ahead if you're delayed.
2. Shake hand firmly.
3. Try to smile and show confidence.
4. Ask questions and show interest in the job.
5. Be polite, listen carefully, and speak clearly.

DON'Ts
1. Don't panic. (Breathe deeply and remember your good points.)
2. Don't slouch or look bored.
(Stand and sit straight; make eye contact.)
3. Don't smoke or chew gum.
4. Don't give one-word answers or say you don't care what you do.

Look at these ads for job openings.

Computer Operator: Expanding data-processing department needs an operator with two years of AS400 experience to handle daily operations. Send résumé to: Personnel Director, American Diversified, 485 Cortlandt Street, Pittsburgh, PA 15620.

Sales-Matsuda of Tokyo: Opportunities available for salesperson in fashionable boutique. Fax résumé and references to: (412) 531-9898 Attention N.C.

Dental Receptionist: Part-time. Bilingual Spanish/English. Mature, bright. Respond with qualifications and salary requirements. Larkin Agency, 254 23rd Street, Pittsburgh, PA 15620.

COVER LETTER

MAKE A GOOD FIRST IMPRESSION:
- Type the letter neatly on good stationery.
- Check for spelling mistakes. Use a dictionary if you are not sure of a word, or use a computer spelling-checker.
- Follow standard, business-letter format. Address the letter and envelope clearly.

421 Lafayette Drive, Apt. 317
St. Paul, MN 55105

April 8, 1996

Personnel Director
Continental Computer Corp.
935 Watson Avenue
St. Paul, MN 55101

Dear Personnel Director:

I am responding to your ad for a Customer Service Representative Trainee in the *Tribune* of Sunday, April 7, 1996.

I have excellent communication skills and I enjoy speaking to people. As you will see from my enclosed résumé, I have experience with several computer systems and computerized order processing.

I would appreciate the opportunity to discuss my qualifications with you. You can reach me at (612) 328-2174.

Sincerely yours,

Peter Meyers

Peter Meyers
Enclosure

Exercise 1

Look at the three ads with a partner. Take turns telling which job you would apply for and why.

Exercise 2

Write a letter applying for one of the three jobs.

Thursday, September 4

BATTLE OF SHERIDAN STREET

BY MARVIN ROTHSTEIN

Police and Housing Authority officials had to turn back again yesterday when they tried to talk to Mrs. Florence Hamilton. They estimated that at least 20 of Mrs. Hamiliton's dogs (the exact number of dogs living with Mrs. Hamilton is not known) guarded both the front and back doors of her house at 875 Sheridan Street in the city's East Side section.

City officials were hoping to speak to the 83-year-old widow, who is still refusing to leave her home. Every other house in an area of several city blocks around Mrs. Hamilton's house has been demolished.

The Housing Authority plans to build a low-income housing project in the area. All of the other residents agreed to move when the authority offered to relocate them to new apartments in the Hillside section.

Police wanted to use stronger methods to remove Mrs. Hamilton and her dogs from their house, but public opinion has forced them to take a more cautious approach.

Conitnued on Page B3

CHANNEL 7 NEWSDESK

Katy Zahn: We have two reports tonight on that continuing story from Sheridan Street. First, let's go to reporter Alan Nelson at City Hall.

REPORT 1

Alan: Thanks, Katy. Well, right now, the City Housing Authority isn't working on anything except the "Battle of Sheridan Street." It's one woman and her pets versus City Hall, and so far she's winning. Ms. Hilda Martinez, the director of the Housing Authority, has agreed to talk with us. Ms. Martinez, has the situation changed since yesterday?

Martinez: No, Alan, it hasn't. Mrs. Hamilton is still in her house, and she still refuses to talk to us.

Alan: What are you going to do?

Martinez: It's a difficult situation. We'd like her to come out peacefully. The police don't intend to arrest her, but she's a very stubborn woman!

Alan: Stubborn? Well, it **is** her home.

Martinez: Yes, and it's been her home for a long time, I know. But nobody else refused to move. You see, we're going to build 400 apartments in that area. We expect to have about 1,200 people living there when the project is finished. You have to balance that against one person and a pack of dogs.

Alan: But Mrs. Hamilton was born in that house, and she is trying to give a home to the homeless dogs of this city.

Martinez: Of course. But we have promised to relocate her and one of her dogs to a modern apartment in a senior-citizens project. The other dogs will go to the ASPCA.

Alan: So, what happens next?

Martinez: We can't wait forever. We want the ASPCA to take all the dogs first. Then we hope to talk to Mrs. Hamilton and convince her to move. We have to do something soon.

Alan: Thank you, Ms. Martinez.... Live from City Hall, this has been Alan Nelson for Channel 7 Newsdesk. And now to Cindy Wong, who is with Mrs. Florence Hamilton at her home on Sheridan Street.

🎧 Listening

Listen to Report 2, Cindy Wong's interview with Mrs. Hamilton, and answer the following question: What does Mrs. Hamilton want?

Exercise 1

"…the other residents agreed to move…" *Agreed to move* is an example of a verb + *to* + another verb.

Read the newspaper article and Alan Nelson's report again and pick out other examples of verbs with *to* and another verb.

Exercise 2

Write five sentences about your plans/intentions/expectations/hopes for the next five years.

Sending a card

Greeting cards are big business in the United States. Millions of cards are sent every year, and you can buy cards for every special occasion—or for no particular occasion at all. You can send cards for Christmas, New Year's, Easter, birthdays, engagements, weddings, births, Valentine's Day, Mother's Day, Father's Day, Halloween, Thanksgiving, illness, graduation, promotion, or just friendship.

For Your Wedding

Best wishes on your wedding!

Dear Linda and Max,
We were delighted to get the news of your marriage. We have to admit—we were surprised to find out that you had eloped! We hope you'll call us soon. We're anxious to hear from you!
Best wishes,
Alice and Brian

Happy Birthday!

It was great to see you in April. Come visit again soon.
Happy Birthday!
Love,
Aunt Mary and Uncle Jacob

In Sympathy

With sincere sympathy in your time of sorrow.

I was so sorry to hear about your dad's passing. It's difficult to put into words how much he meant to me. I remember when he was our Little League coach. He was always ready to help me develop my abilities, and he was always willing to listen to me. Please express my condolences to your family.

Reggie

Exercise 1

sorry to hear…, delighted to get, etc., are examples of the structure: adjective + *to* + verb. Using this structure and some news you've heard recently, write your own greeting card.

WEDDING ANNIVERSARIES

THE TRADITIONAL GIFTS FOR EACH ANNIVERSARY:

1st	paper	25th	silver
2nd	cotton	30th	pearl
3rd	leather	35th	jade
4th	linen	40th	ruby
5th	wood	45th	sapphire
10th	tin	50th	gold
15th	crystal	55th	emerald
20th	china	60th	diamond

Exercise 2

Suggest a suitable gift for each anniversary above.
2nd anniversary   cotton
You could give a tablecloth or some towels.

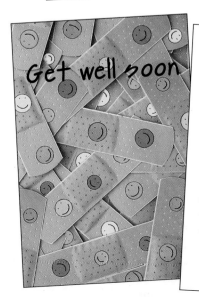

Get well soon

Hope you're on your feet again soon!

Dear Matthew,
I was really upset to hear about your accident. It sounded terrible! You're lucky to have only one broken leg! I hope to see you soon.
Love,
Rachel

Marriage counseling

Jonathan and Barbara Weiner have been married for nearly 15 years. They have two children, Gary, aged 11, and Debbie, 9. During the last couple of years, Jonathan and Barbara haven't been very happy. They argue all the time. Barbara's sister advised them to go to a marriage counselor. A marriage counselor helps married couples to talk about their problems and to solve them, if possible. Sometimes Jonathan and Barbara meet with the counselor separately, and other times they meet with her together. This is Jonathan and Barbara's third session with Dr. Joyce Sisters, the counselor.

BARBARA'S SESSION

Dr. Sisters: Oh, come in, Barbara. Have a seat. Didn't Jonathan come?

Barbara: Yes, he's waiting outside. He didn't want to come this week, but…well, I persuaded him to come.

Dr. Sisters: I see. How have things been going?

Barbara: Oh, about the same. We still seem to have fights all the time.

Dr. Sisters: What do you fight about?

Barbara: What *don't* we fight about, you mean? We fight about everything. He's so inconsiderate.

Dr. Sisters: How so?

Barbara: Well, I'll give you an example. You know, when the children started school, I wanted to go back to teaching again. So I got a job. Well, anyway, by the time I've picked Gary and Debbie up at my sister's house—she picks them up at school—I only get home about half an hour before Jonathan.

Dr. Sisters: Yes?

Barbara: Well, when he gets home, he expects me to run around and get dinner on the table. He never does anything in the house.

Dr. Sisters: Hmm.

Barbara: And last Friday! He invited three of his friends to come over for a drink. He didn't tell me to expect them. I don't think that's right, do you?

Dr. Sisters: Barbara, I'm not here to pass judgment. I'm here to listen.

Barbara: I'm sorry. And he's so messy. He's worse than the kids. I always have to remind him to pick up his clothes. He just throws them on the floor. After all, I'm not his mother. And I have my own career. Actually, I think that's part of the trouble. You see, I make more money than he does.

🎧 Listening

Listen to Jonathan's session with Dr. Sisters.

Answer the following questions:

Why did Barbara have to force Jonathan to come to the session?

How does Jonathan feel about Barbara's job?

Why don't Jonathan and Barbara talk much?

Why won't Barbara let the children ride their bikes to school?

Exercise 1

Barbara's sister advised them to go…

There are six other sentences like this on this page.

Underline them or write them out.

Exercise 2

They're very tired. They can't talk.
They're too tired to talk.

Continue.

1. They're very young. They shouldn't ride bikes to school.
2. He's very old. He can't go to work.
3. We were very surprised. We couldn't say anything.
4. She's very sick. She shouldn't go out.

Exercise 3

Discuss Jonathan and Barbara's problems in groups. What would you advise him/her to do? Who do you think is right?

At home with the Baldwins

The Baldwin family is like many contemporary American families: both parents work. Evan is a lawyer, Lynn is a photographer, Zach, 12, is in seventh grade, and Chloe, 8, is in fourth grade.

7:30 AM

Evan: Zachary, are you ready for breakfast?
Zach: No, Dad. I have to make my bed first.
Evan: OK, but hurry up. Mom's making hot cereal. By the way, what do you want for lunch today?
Zach: Can I have turkey? I'm tired of tuna.
Evan: No problem.

Chloe: Mom, I can't find my red sweater, and I want to wear it today.
Lynn: I think it's in the hamper. I'm going to do the laundry later, so you can wear it tomorrow. Can I make a suggestion? Why don't you wear your pink sweater today?
Chloe: Oh, all right. Can you do my hair now?
Lynn: In a minute. I have to get Zach. His breakfast is getting cold.
Chloe: Is Daddy making dinner tonight?
Lynn: Uh-huh.
Chloe: Can we have spaghetti and meatballs?
Lynn: OK. I have to make a shopping list. I'm going to do the shopping on my way home. Would you check to see if we have any spaghetti, please?

7:30 PM

Lynn: Zachary, have you done your homework yet?
Zach: Yeah, Mom. I did it right after karate class.
Lynn: Great. Let me look at it.
Zach: Here, Mom. Here's my homework.
Lynn: You did a good job, Zach. Did you have to do anything else?
Zach: Uh, I also had to do some reading in my history book. And I had to do a crossword puzzle for science. It was easy, though.
Lynn: You're sure you didn't make any mistakes?
Zach: Yup. I'm positive.

Evan: Hey, Chloe. What are you doing?
Chloe: I'm making a picture for the story I wrote in school today.
Evan: Oh, yeah? Terrific. Can I see it? It's very pretty. I like the colors.
Chloe: Thanks, Dad.
Evan: Chloe, go look in the kitchen. Is Mom making coffee?
Chloe: Uh, no, Daddy, she's doing the dishes.
Evan: Oh. I guess I can wait a few minutes. I have to make a call.
Chloe: Are you calling Grandma?
Evan: No. It's a business call. I told someone I'd call him before 8:00 tonight. I hate to do business from home, but he's a special case.

Do	MAKE
the shopping	a scene
work	plans
homework	coffee
housework	a suggestion
the cleaning	a call
the ironing	a decision
the dishes	a bed
one's hair	an effort
something interesting	an excuse
a good job	a mistake
business	a noise
errands	a profit
a favor	dinner
a puzzle	trouble
the laundry	a list

Look at this:
"Have you *done* your homework yet?"
"I'm *doing* the dishes."
"I have to *make* my bed first."
"Is Dad *making* dinner tonight?"

Exercise 1

I always do my homework.
I made my bed this morning.

Write ten sentences, five with *do* and five with *make*.

Exercise 2

Discuss: Do you think men and women should share the housekeeping chores and parenting duties? Do you think children should have to do chores?

Sounding polite

We use words like *please, thank you,* and *you're welcome* to be polite. But we also communicate politeness with our voice using stress, intonation, and tone.

STRESS is how loud syllables or words are.

INTONATION is the way the voice rises and falls.

TONE is the manner of our expression.

Listen to these sentences. The words are the same, but the message is different: the first is polite; the second is not.

Polite: Could you hold the door open, please?

Impolite: Could you hold the door open, please?

Listening 1

Listen to these sentences. Write *P* for polite, *I* for impolite.

. . . Would you turn down the radio, please?

. . . Would you turn down the radio, please?

. . . Would you turn down the radio, please?

. . . Open the door, please.

. . . Open the door, please.

. . . Open the door, please.

. . . Could you make a copy of this?

. . . Could you make a copy of this?

. . . Could you make a copy of this?

. . . Can I use your stapler?

. . . Can I use your stapler?

. . . Can I use your stapler?

. . . Would you please take our picture?

. . . Would you please take our picture?

. . . Would you please take our picture?

. . . Can I get change for a dollar?

. . . Can I get change for a dollar?

. . . Can I get change for a dollar?

Listening 2

Listen to the conversations. The sentence below each picture is what the speaker will say next. Predict how the speaker will say the sentence.

Could you walk a little faster, please?

Can I use that pen?

Would you mind turning off the TV?

Listen again and check your answers.

Polite requests

A: Mike?
B: Yeah?
A: Close the door, will you? It's freezing in here.
B: Sure. I'm sorry.

shut the window/cold
open the door/very hot

C: Karen?
D: Hmm?
C: Lend me 50 cents. I left my purse in the office.
D: Oh, OK. Here.
C: Thanks.

$5/wallet $1/handbag

E: Excuse me. Could you pass the sugar?
F: Of course. There you are.
E: Thank you very much.

cream   salt   pepper

G: Do you need some help?
H: Oh, thank you. Would you mind putting my suitcase up on the rack?
G: Not at all. There you go.
H: Oh, thank you so much. You're very kind.

bag/under the seat
shopping bag/rack

I: Excuse me. It's stuffy in here. Do you mind if I open the window?
J: No, I don't mind at all. I'd like some fresh air too.

cold/close/cold too
feel hot/open/stuffy too

K: Excuse me, Lorraine. Could I ask you something?
L: Sure, Wendy. What is it?
K: Can I have the day off next Friday?
L: Well, we're very busy now. Is it important?
K: Yeah, it is, really. It's my cousin's wedding.
L: Oh, well, of course you can!

Tuesday/sister
Wednesday/nephew
Thursday/niece

M: Can I help you, ma'am?
N: I beg your pardon?
M: Can I help you, ma'am?
N: Oh. No, no thanks. I'm just looking.

Sir/Pardon?
Miss/Excuse me?

O: Good morning.
P: Good morning. I wonder if you can help me. I'm looking for a Father's Day present for my father.
O: Have you thought about a nice tie?
P: Hmm…maybe. Could you show me some of your ties?

wedding/cousin/some towels

Q: Excuse me.
R: Yes?
Q: I wonder if you'd mind handing me one of those cans of peas—on the top shelf. I can't reach it.
R: Oh, sure. There you are.
Q: Thank you very much.

box of cornflakes   package of pasta
roll of paper towels   bottle of oil

A trip to Los Angeles

James Hall has a new job with Lemon Computers in Philadelphia. He's 22 and just out of college. As part of his training, he has to spend six weeks at company headquarters near Los Angeles. It's his first business trip, and he's packing his suitcase. He lives with his parents, and his mother is helping him.

James: OK. Where's the tag?
Mrs. Hall: What tag, hon?
James: The name tag that the airline gave me to put on the suitcase. Oh, here it is.
Mrs. Hall: Now, do you have the key?
James: What key?
Mrs. Hall: The key to lock the suitcase, of course.
James: It's in the lock, Mom. There's nothing to worry about. There's plenty of time.
Mrs. Hall: Have you forgotten anything?
James: I hope not.
Mrs. Hall: And you have a safe pocket for your traveler's checks?
James: Yes, they're in my inside coat pocket.
Mrs. Hall: Do you have a book to read on the plane?
James: Yes, it's in my briefcase.

Mrs. Hall: What about small change to make phone calls?
James: Check. I have a pocketful of coins.

Mrs. Hall: Is there someone to meet you in Los Angeles?
James: No, Mom. I'll rent a car and go to a hotel near the office. They suggested the Hollywood Inn.
Mrs. Hall: Do you have a reservation?
James: I hope so. I asked them to make it—the hotel reservation, I mean. I reserved the car myself.
Mrs. Hall: Well, take care of yourself and be good. Call us tonight.
James: Thanks, Mom. I will.
Mrs. Hall: Oh, I nearly forgot! Here's some gum to chew on the plane— you know, when it's coming down.
James: Oh, Mom. Don't worry. I'll be all right. I'll see you next month.

Mrs. Hall: Jimmy, haven't you finished packing yet?
James: No, Mom, but it's all right. There isn't much to do.
Mrs. Hall: Well, I'll give you a hand. Oh. There isn't much room left. Is there anywhere to put your shaving kit?
James: Yeah, sure. It'll go in here. Now, I have three more shirts to pack. They'll go on top, but there's another pair of shoes to get in…
Mrs. Hall: Put them here, one on each side. There. OK, I think we can close it now.

Exercise 1

James made a list. Look at it.

He remembered to pack his shirts.
He forgot to pack his raincoat.

Continue.

Exercise 2

Discuss: Why do you think Mrs. Hall was so worried? Do you think she should have been?

🎧 Listening 1: At the airport

James is at the Air USA terminal at the airport. He's already checked in. He's been through the security check, and he's gone to the gate to wait for his flight. Listen to the announcements. Look at the screen below, look at the example, and complete the chart in the same way.

AIR USA

FLIGHT	DESTINATION	GATE	DEPARTS
932	Syracuse	14	3:25
217			
558			
563			
67			
811			

🎧 Listening 2: In flight

James is now on the plane. Listen to the announcements and answer these questions.

1. What's the pilot's name? What are they waiting for? How long will the delay be? When will they arrive in Los Angeles?
2. What kind of plane is it? How fast is it going? Where is the plane? How hot is it in Los Angeles? What's the weather like? Why should the passengers keep their seat belts fastened?
3. What's the plane beginning to do? What should the passengers do?
4. What should the passengers do? Who should they see if they have questions?

BEVERAGES ON THE PLANE

Flight Attendant: Something to drink, sir?
James: Yeah…uh…yes, thanks. I'd like some club soda.
Attendant: With lime or without?
James: With lime, please…. Uh, how much is that?
Attendant: It's complimentary. The soft drinks are free.
James: Great. Uh, will you be serving dinner soon?
Attendant: Sure. As soon as we finish the beverage service.
James: Oh good. What is it?
Attendant: We have a choice today of lasagna or chicken.
James: Thanks. Uh, would you mind giving me some more peanuts? I'm getting kind of hungry.
Attendant: Not at all, sir, here you go.

IN-FLIGHT QUESTIONNAIRE

Attendant: Excuse me, sir. Would you mind filling out this questionnaire?
James: What's it about?
Attendant: It's a survey.
James: OK, I'll fill it out.

AIR USA PASSENGER QUESTIONNAIRE

Please take a few minutes to fill out this questionnaire and return it to your flight attendant. Thank you for helping us serve you better.

Date_____

Flight No._____

From_____

To_____

How many flights do you take in a year?_____

What cities do you travel to mostly?_____
_____
_____

Do you fly most often for business or for pleasure?
_____

Why did you choose to fly Air USA today?
_____

AUTO RENTAL

Customer Service Representative: May I help you?
James: Yes. I have a reservation. My name is James Hall. My confirmation number is 75088821.
Rep.: 75088821. Just a moment, sir. Ah, yes, I have it. OK, I just need some information. That's Hall, James. Address?
James: 427 Longwood Avenue, Philadelphia, PA 19119.
Rep.: Are you here for business or for pleasure?
James: Business. Uh, I'm supposed to get the corporate discount.
Rep.: Oh, yes, I see it here. And how long will you need the car?
James: One week.
Rep.: All right. May I see your driver's license and a major credit card?
James: Just a moment…oh, no! I left my driver's license in Philadelphia!

Money

U.S. AND CANADIAN MONEY

Read the text and compare with currency in your country.

U.S. treasury bills (*greenbacks* in slang) are different from those in most countries. They're all the same color and size. Most people in the United States do not want to change either the look or the feel of their money. For example, the dollar bill is now a pretty small unit for a bill. A few years ago, a dollar coin was introduced, but it was unpopular. Because American bills look the same, cashiers will often say "out of twenty" when you give them a $20 bill, so that there won't be any dispute later.

In Canada, the bills are different sizes and colors. One Canadian dollar is a coin and two-dollar bills are common. Canadians call the dollar coin a *loony* because the bird on the coin is a loon. *Loony* is also a slang name for *crazy*.

🎧 Listening: Buying with a credit card

MacGizmos INC. **TAMPA FL.** Time: 12:34 pm **Date:** 11/30 Catalog number: _____ **TELEPHONE ORDER** Customer's Name: _____ Address: _____ _____ Zip Code: _____ ☐ MasterCard ☐ VISA ☐ DISCOVER ☐ AMERICAN Card Card Number: ▯▯▯▯ ▯▯▯▯ ▯▯▯▯ ▯▯▯▯ Expiration date: _____ Name on card: _____ Total: $ _____ Send by: ☐Surface ☐Air ☐Courier ***Thank you for shopping with us!***	Credit cards can be used in millions of locations worldwide. They can be used for buying things by telephone. This is useful if you want to buy things from another country. Listen to the conversation and complete the credit card slip on the left.

CREDIT CARD NUMBERS

Why can't people just order goods by phone, with invented credit card numbers? Credit cards have between 15- and 20-digit card numbers. In fact, with just an eight-digit number a credit card company could have 100 million different cardholders. The long number is a security device. For example, American Express cards have a 15-digit number. If you write down any 15-digit number, the chance of it being an actual credit card number is one in 90 million. MasterCards can have 20 digits. The chance of matching a real number is about one in one and a half trillion!

ATMS (AUTOMATIC TELLER MACHINES)

Answer these questions:
Do you have an ATM card?
How often do you use it?
Have you ever used it in a foreign country?
Is your ATM card a separate card, or is it a combined credit and ATM card?

Look at these American ATM screens. They show someone withdrawing $200 from their checking account.

Number the screens in the correct sequence from 1 to 7.

a

b

c

d

e

f

g

Are ATM instructions the same in your country?
Can you get any other services from an ATM?

Listening: Bargaining

Lynn Bunker is at a flea market in a small Connecticut town. She's just seen a glass bowl at one of the stands. She collects American glass objects made during the 1930s. She's interested in buying the bowl. Listen to her conversation with the owner of the stand, and answer these questions.

1. How much does he say it's worth?
2. How much is he asking for it?
3. What does *buck* mean?
4. He suggests five different prices. Write them down.
5. She makes three offers. Write them down.

SOME SAYINGS IN ENGLISH ABOUT MONEY:

"A penny saved is a penny earned."
BENJAMIN FRANKLIN

Do you save money? Are you saving for anything right now? What?

Do you keep your money
(a) in the bank?
(b) in a safe?
(c) in a book?
(d) under the bed?
(e) in the refrigerator?

Do you have a bank account? Do you have a checking account or a savings account? What's the interest rate? If your account was overdrawn, how much would the bank charge you?

"Buy now; pay later."

Have you ever bought anything on credit? What? Did you pay a deposit? Do you think it's a good idea?

Do you have a credit card? Which one? (Visa? American Express? Diner's Club? MasterCard?)

When you pay cash, do you ask for a discount? Do you usually get it?

"A fool and his money are soon parted."

Where do you carry your spending money?
(a) in a purse
(b) in a wallet
(c) in a pocket
If you keep it in a pocket, which pocket do you keep it in?
(a) inside pocket of coat/jacket
(b) breast pocket of coat/jacket
(c) side pocket of coat/jacket
(d) back pocket of pants
(e) front pocket of pants

Have you ever had your pocket picked?

When you stay in a hotel, do you hide your money? Where?
(a) in your suitcase
(b) under the mattress
(c) in the pillow
(d) in a book
(e) somewhere else

Is gambling legal or illegal in your city/state/province/country? Do people bet? What do they bet on?
(a) cards
(b) horse racing
(c) dog racing
(d) football/soccer/boxing/other sport
(e) national lottery
(f) something else

"Neither a borrower nor a lender be."
FROM *HAMLET*
BY WILLIAM SHAKESPEARE

Have you ever borrowed money from anyone? Who from? How much?

Have you ever lent money to anyone? Who to? How much?

Are you in debt at the moment (i.e., do you owe anyone any money)?

Does anyone owe you any money? Who? How much?

"The customer is always right."

Have you bought anything this week? What?
What did it cost? Was it worth it?
Was it new or used?
Was it a bargain? Did you get a receipt?

Have you ever returned anything you had bought? What? Where?
Did you get your money back, a new article, a different article, or credit for a future purchase?

KIDNAPPED!

BY JULIE MENDOZA

CHICAGO, June 28—Billy Simpson, the ten-year-old son of multimillionaire business executive Jules Simpson, was apparently kidnapped yesterday from his family's estate in a suburb near here. The boy was fishing alone at the pond, about a half-mile from his house, when the kidnapping took place.

Mr. Simpson, who was not available for comment, is the founder of the J Mart chain discount stores. His wife, Emily, had been in Paris and was flying back in the Simpsons' private jet when word of the kidnapping reached her.

Police spokesperson Lisa Galacko says they have no suspects yet, but they are "pursuing certain leads." The police are combing the area near the estate and (continued on page B21)

KIDNAPPERS SURRENDER!
SIMPSON BOY SAFE

BY JULIE MENDOZA

CHICAGO, June 29—Billy Simpson, kidnapped two days ago from the grounds of his home, was returned safely to his parents, Jules and Emily Simpson. No ransom was paid.

Looking bruised and beaten, Thomas Ahern, 23, and Steven Cobb, 25, both of Chicago, surrendered today to Chicago police. They turned themselves in and were immediately arrested and taken to the hospital for treatment of various wounds. It isn't clear yet how they received the wounds, but police spokesman Lisa Galacko said the two were not injured by the police.

(continued on page B15)

ABN EVENING NEWS

Young Billy Simpson's ordeal ended abruptly when the two kidnappers returned the boy safely to the Simpson home earlier today. Police Commissioner Ben Hawkins has spoken to the boy and the two kidnappers. We're waiting for the commissioner to arrive to begin his press conference. Ah, here he is now.

Hawkins: Good evening. As you know, the Simpson boy was returned safe and sound at two o'clock this afternoon. The kidnappers were planning to force Mr. Simpson to pay $10 million in ransom for the boy's safe return.

Reporter: How exactly did they kidnap Billy?

Hawkins: Cobb and Ahern managed to tunnel under a security fence and found Billy fishing alone at the pond. They forced Billy to go with them through the tunnel. Then they made him get into their car and lie down on the back seat. They took him to a remote, wooded area. They made the boy believe that there were wild animals in the area, and that he should stay with them to be safe. That's how they forced him to stay with them.

Reporter: Did they harm Billy?

Hawkins: No. After the first hour at the camp, they let him walk about freely. They were sure that he wouldn't go far; he was too scared. In fact, they made him collect wood for a fire, and he had a great time. That's when he accidentally hit Cobb in the head with a log.

Reporter: Is that why Cobb looks so terrible?

Hawkins: Well, in part. Billy also got Ahern to go berry-picking with him. Ahern didn't realize he was walking through poison ivy; that's why Ahern's got all those rashes on him.

Reporter: Why didn't Billy get rashes?

Hawkins: He's not affected by poison ivy. But Ahern certainly is!

Reporter: What else happened to Cobb and Ahern?

Hawkins: Well, this morning, Ahern and Cobb allowed Billy to play near the campsite. Billy wanted to play Tarzan, so he climbed a tree. But he was afraid to climb down. He made Ahern climb up to help him, but Ahern fell off and nearly broke his leg. In his hurry to help his buddy, Cobb tripped over a rock and landed in the campfire. He got burns over 20% of his body. In the meantime, Billy got down from the tree by himself. That's when Ahern and Cobb decided to give up. They drove Billy back to the estate, and asked the Simpsons to get them medical attention.

Exercise 1

Underline examples in the story of:

force allow	someone to do something
make let	someone do something

Exercise 2

When I was younger, my parents made me go to bed early.
When I was younger, my parents didn't let me go out at night.

Write true sentences about when you were younger.

Compare your sentences with those of other students.

Exercise 3

What do you think parents should let/allow children to do? What should they make/force them to do? Why?

A: What are you doing tomorrow night?
B: Nothing. Why?
A: Well, do you like music?
B: Yes, I do—very much.
A: Which do you like better—country or jazz?
B: I like both, as a matter of fact.
A: Well, Joe Ed Davis is playing at the Hoot 'N Holler. Would you like to go?
B: Yeah, great! He's one of my favorites!

C: Hey, Carla, look…. They have a fabulous selection of jeans!
D: Oh, yeah! And they have my size!
C: Yeah, but only in Bee Cees and Guest.
D: Yeah. Hmm. I don't like either one of them very much. I really wanted some Rustler's.
C: But they don't have them in your size. Try a pair of Bee Cees.
D: No, I'd rather find some Rustler's somewhere else.

E: Well, what movie do you want to see?
F: *A Moment of Peace* is at the MCM 2. I'd like to see that.
E: I'd rather not. Let's see *All's Fair*.
F: Oh, no! The reviews were terrible.
E: But it sounds like fun. *A Moment of Peace* is in French and I really don't want to read subtitles.
F: Then how about *California Sunset*?
E: I'd rather not. I can't stand Steve Newman.
F: Well, you choose then.
E: You know, I'd much rather stay home and rent a video.

G: What do you feel like having?
H: I don't know. There isn't much choice, is there?
G: No, not really. What would you rather have? Chicken a la king or spaghetti and meatballs?
H: I can't make up my mind. Uh—I'd just like a tuna fish sandwich.
G: We can look at the regular menu, if you'd like.
H: No, it's not worth it. I'll have the spaghetti.

Exercise

You and a friend are trying to decide what to do for the evening: stay home and rent a video, go dancing, go hear some music, eat dinner in a restaurant, or go to the movies. Have a conversation, discussing your preferences. Decide what to do.

This Week in Denver
Jazz, Funk, Country, Bluegrass

Blaze Foley and **The Ramblers** (country)
Billy's on Third (861-9540), Wed. & Thurs.

Jo Ed Davis and **The Harris County Line Band**
(bluegrass) Hoot 'N Holler (499-3773), Tues. –Thurs.

M.G. Mallet (rap)
The Ritz (561-7799), Thurs.–Sat.

Gloria Esterhaze in concert. (pop)
Mermorial Coliseum (485-5000), Sat. 8 PM.

Mile High Trio (jazz)
Blakely's (870-9434), Wed.–Sun. 9:00 and 11:00

Try our lunchtime special:

Mushroom Soup
Split Pea Soup

Chicken a la King
Spaghetti and Meatballs

Apple Pie a la Mode
Chocolate Layer Cake

ELITE CAFÉ
1224 DEXTER AVENUE
(1/4 MILE FROM RITZ SIXPLEX)

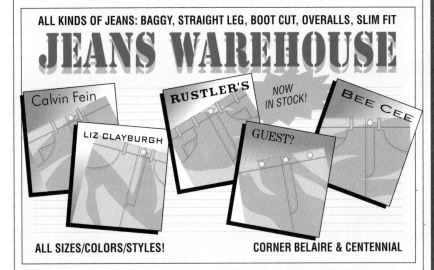

ALL KINDS OF JEANS: BAGGY, STRAIGHT LEG, BOOT CUT, OVERALLS, SLIM FIT

JEANS WAREHOUSE

Calvin Fein   LIZ CLAYBURGH   RUSTLER'S   NOW IN STOCK!   GUEST?   BEE CEE

ALL SIZES/COLORS/STYLES!   CORNER BELAIRE & CENTENNIAL

100% COTTON SHIRTS CUSTOM MADE!

ONLY $49⁹⁵

ORDER NOW WHILE THEY LAST!
WOMEN'S AND MEN'S STYLES

Available in white/cream/beige/light blue/gray/black/dark green/burgundy/pink. When ordering, state color preference and alternative choices.

Men's sizes 14–17-1/2 (neck) • Women's sizes 32–40 (bust)

Name _____
Address _____
City _____ State _____ Zip Code _____
Please send me _____ shirts. Size _____
Color: 1st choice _____
     2nd choice _____
     3rd choice _____
I enclose _____ plus $1.50 for shipping.

FASHION BY MAIL • P.O. Box 5500, Boulder, CO 80301

Movie Listings
Denver area

MCM 1 & 2
Shudder! (PG) 8:00, 10:25
A Moment of Peace (R) 6:45, 8:30, 10:00
(French—English subtitles)

Paramount
All's Fair (R) 5:15, 7:45, 10:00
Steve DeWit, Melissa Marks

Ritz Sixplex
California Sunset (PG-13) 7:30, 9:10, 11:05
Steve Newman, Gloria Gusto
What a Night! (PG-13) 8:00, 9:40
Rod de Biro, Alexis Riddler
Talk! Talk! (PG-13) 6:30, 8:10, 9:50
Carole Mankind, Walt Stultz
Are You Lonesome Tonight? (PG-13)
7:15, 8:40, 10.05
Hank Garvey, Lois Frank

Earth Day

Today is Earth Day, and we're here in Central Park for the big cleanup and celebration. We asked some of the people who turned out today what they think we ought to do to help the environment.

Well, I think we'd better do something to protect the tropical rain forests before they're all gone. You know, rain forests only make up like two percent of the Earth's surface, but over half the world's wild plant, animal, and insect species live there. One out of every four pharmaceuticals comes from a plant in a tropical rain forest. We ought to support organizations involved in rain forest conservation, like the Rain Forest Action Network in San Francisco.

The most important thing to me is to save and care for all the wildlife in the world. Did you know that by the year 2000, 20% of all Earth's species could be lost forever? And we'd better not save only the mammals—we ought to be concerned about the insects, fish, amphibians, reptiles, and plants. I think the governments of the world had better get together and do something.

I'm really worried about the quality of the air we breathe. Cars cause a lot of the air pollution and everybody ought to do whatever possible to stop it, you know. For example, people ought to drive together or use public transportation—that would keep millions of pounds of pollution out of the atmosphere. People ought to buy cars that get good gas mileage and keep them tuned up and running well. The more gas a car uses, the more pollution it emits. We'd all better support

the development and use of cars that use alternative energy sources—like electric cars, solar-powered cars, and cars that run on methane gas.

We'd better not take the water we have for granted in this country. Every day, we consume 450 billion gallons of water! We get this water from our rivers, lakes, and streams, or from groundwater, and we have been careless about how we've treated our water sources. We ought to take better care of the groundwater and keep it safe from pollutants—especially chemicals that people pour down their drains without thinking or gasoline leaks from underground storage tanks. We'd also better start conserving water.

Exercise 1

Discuss: What do you think people ought to do to help the environment?

Exercise 2

Find words that mean:
1. controlled use of natural resources like air, water, fuel
2. warm-blooded animals
3. wild plants and animals
4. a sub-class of living things
5. drugs
6. maintain by supplying money or other assistance
7. gives off
8. other
9. point of origin
10. use up

"This is your captain, John Cook, speaking. We've reached our cruising altitude and I've just turned off the *Fasten seat belt* sign. Our estimated time of arrival in Anchorage is 1:00 AM, so we've got a long flight ahead of us. I hope you enjoy it. Our flight attendants will be serving dinner shortly. Thank you."

It was Christmas Eve 1959. A lot of the passengers on the nearly full plane were traveling home to spend the holidays with their families. It was a smooth and quiet flight. The flight attendants had just finished picking up the trays and were in the galley putting things away when the first buzzers sounded. One of the flight attendants went down the aisle to check. When she came back she looked surprised. "It's amazing," she said. "Even on a smooth flight like this two people have gotten sick."

Twenty minutes later nearly half the passengers were sick—violently sick. Several were moaning and groaning, some were doubled up in pain, and two were unconscious. Fortunately, there was a doctor on board, and he was helping the flight attendants. He came to the galley and said, "I'd better speak to the pilot. This is a severe case of food poisoning. I think we'd better land as soon as possible." "What caused it?" asked one of the flight attendants. "Well," replied the

doctor, "I had the beef for dinner, and I'm fine. The passengers who chose the fish are sick."

The flight attendant led him to the cockpit. The door was jammed. Together they pushed it open. The captain was lying unconscious behind the door. The copilot was slumped across the controls, and the engineer was trying to revive him. The doctor quickly examined the two men. "Can you land the plane?" the doctor asked the engineer. "Me? No, I'm not a pilot. We've got to revive them!" he replied. "The plane's on automatic pilot. We're OK for a couple of hours." "They could be out for a long time," said the doctor. "I'd better contact ground control," said the engineer. "Maybe you should make an announcement and try to find out if there's a pilot on board," the doctor suggested. "We can't do that!" the flight attendant said. "It'll cause a general panic."

Suddenly she remembered something. "One of the passengers… I overheard him saying that he'd been a pilot. I'll get him." She found the man and asked him to come to the galley. "Didn't you say you used to be a pilot?" she asked. "Yes… why?" She led him to the cockpit. They explained the situation to him. "You mean, you want me to fly the plane?" he asked. "You must be

joking. I was a pilot, but I flew single-engined fighter planes, and that was 15 years ago. This thing's got four engines! Isn't there anybody else?" he asked. "I'm afraid not," said the flight attendant.

The man sat down at the controls. His hands were shaking slightly. The engineer connected him to Air Traffic Control. They told him to keep flying on automatic pilot toward Anchorage and wait for further instructions from an experienced pilot. An hour later, the lights of Anchorage appeared on the horizon. He could see the lights of the runway shining brightly by a lake. Air Traffic Control told him to keep circling until the fuel gauge registered almost empty. This gave him a chance to get used to handling the controls.

🎧 **Listening**

Listen to the end of the story and answer these questions:
What were the flight attendants and doctor doing?
How long did the plane circle?
What caused the bump that shook the plane?
What vehicles were on the runway waiting for the plane to land?
Was the landing a success?
What did the man who was piloting the plane ask the air-traffic controller?

Anita Jameson and Steve Weaver are antique dealers. They have a very successful business. They travel around the country buying antique furniture and paintings from flea markets, antique stores, and elderly people. Steve has just come out of a little antique store, and he seems very excited.

Steve: Anita, we're in luck! There's a painting in there, a landscape. It's a good one. I thought it might be valuable, so I took a good look at the signature. It isn't very clear, but I think it may be a Winslow Homer.

Anita: A Winslow Homer?! It can't be! They're all in museums. They're worth a fortune!

Steve: Well, someone found one a couple of years ago. This might be another one. It's dirty, and it isn't in very good condition.

Anita: How much do you think it's worth?

Steve: I don't know, maybe a million; it might even be worth more!

Anita: Be careful, Steve. We'd better use the old trick.

Steve: Yeah, right. There's a chair in the window. It must be worth about $20. I'll offer a hundred bucks for it. She'll be so happy that she won't think about the painting.

Anita: Don't say you want the painting; say you want the frame. OK?

Steve: Fine, you'd better wait in the van. I'd rather do this on my own.

Anita: Uh…Steve, check the signature before you give her a hundred bucks for the chair.

Steve: Don't worry, Anita. I know what I'm doing.

Mrs. Venable: I'll be with you in a minute.

Steve: I'm interested in that chair in the window.

Mrs. Venable: What? That old thing? It's been there for years!

Steve: It has? Uh…it's very nice. I think it could be Victorian.

Mrs. Venable: Really?

Steve: Yes, I think I'm right. I've seen one or two other chairs like it. I think I could get a good price for that in New York. I'll offer you $100.

Mrs. Venable: A hundred dollars! You must be out of your mind!

Steve: No, no. It's a fair price.

Mrs. Venable: Well, then, it's yours.

Steve: There you are then, $100. Good-bye. Oh, by the way, that painting's in a nice frame.

Mrs. Venable: It's a nice picture, honey. Late 19th century, I've heard.

Steve: Oh, no…no, it can't be. I've seen lots like it. It must be 20th century. There's no market for them. Still, I could use the frame.

Mrs. Venable: All right. How much will you give me for it?

Steve: Uh…how about $40?

Mrs. Venable: Oh, no, honey. It must be worth more than that. It came from the big house on the hill.

Speculation

Steve: It did? Let me have another look at it. Yes, the frame really is nice. I'll give you $200.

Mrs. Venable: Oh, my, I don't know what to do. You see, I like that painting myself.

Steve: All right, $250. That's my final offer.

Mrs. Venable: Let's say…$275?

Steve: OK. It's a deal.

Mrs. Venable: Should I wrap it up for you?

Steve: No, no. I have the van outside. It was nice doing business with you. Good-bye!

Mrs. Venable: Bye-bye, honey. Thank you. You come back to see us, you hear?

Mrs. Venable: Beauregard?

Mr. Venable: Yes, darling?

Mrs. Venable: I've sold another one of your imitation Winslow Homers. You'd better bring another one downstairs, if the paint's dry. The young gentleman who bought it seemed very happy with it.

Look at this:

It's certainly…	It must be…
I'm almost certain…	
It's probably…	It could be…
	It may be…
It's possibly…	It might be…
(but a little less possible than *may*)	
It's probably not…	It can't be…
It's definitely not…	It couldn't be…

Exercise 1

It's probably a hundred years old.
It could be a hundred years old.

Rephrase the following sentences.
1. It's definitely not by Leonardo da Vinci.
2. It's probably not a Rembrandt.
3. It's certainly worth over a million dollars.
4. I'm almost certain it's in the Metropolitan Museum now.
5. It's definitely not a Winslow Homer.

Exercise 2

Discuss: Who was the *swindler*?

swindler person who gets money or property from someone through trickery/cheating.

Noisy neighbors

Harriet: *Pssst!* Ozzie! Ozzie! Wake up!

Ozzie: Huh? What? What's the matter? It can't be seven o'clock already!

Harriet: No. It's 1:30. It's those people next door again. Listen!

Ozzie: Oh, yeah. They must be having another party.

Harriet: They must be waking up the whole block. And they have three young children. Those kids couldn't be sleeping through that racket. It's disgusting! Somebody should call the police!

Ozzie: They're all laughing. They must be having a good time. They never invite us, do they?

Harriet: Ozzie!

Ozzie: Yes, dear. What is it now?

Harriet: Listen! They must be leaving.

Ozzie: At last! Maybe we'll get some sleep.

Harriet: I hope so. It's nearly three o'clock. Good night, dear. Oh, no! Now they're having a fight.

Ozzie: That figures. They always have fights after parties.

Harriet: Uh-oh! They must be throwing the dishes again.

Ozzie: No, I think that was a vase, dear, or maybe the TV set—or both!

Harriet: Ozzie! Listen. There's someone in the backyard next door.

Ozzie: Huh? It must be a cat.

Harriet: No, it can't be. It's too loud.

Ozzie: What time is it?

Harriet: It's a quarter to five. Who could it be? I'd better take a look. *Ooh!* It's Howard, and he's carrying a shovel.

Ozzie: Really? You don't think he's killed her, do you?

Harriet: Well, we haven't heard her voice for a while. No, she's probably sleeping.

Ozzie: But what could he be doing at this time of the morning?

Harriet: If he has killed her, he might be burying the body!

Ozzie: What! You don't think so, do you?

Harriet: He couldn't be planting tomatoes, could he? I'm going to ask him what he's doing.

Harriet: Hello there, Howard. You're up bright and early this morning.

Howard: I haven't been to bed yet. We had a party last night. I hope we didn't keep you awake.

Harriet: Oh, no, no. We didn't hear a thing, nothing at all. I slept like a log.

Howard: Well, it was a pretty noisy party. My wife knocked over the kids' hamster cage while we were cleaning up. The poor hamster died. I'm just burying him before the kids wake up.

Exercise

What do you think your parents/brothers/ sisters/friends are doing right now?

If you think you know what they are doing, answer with:
They must be doing this.
They couldn't be doing that.
They're probably doing this.

If you don't know, use:
They could/may/might be doing this.
or:
They're probably doing this.

What about the president of the United States/your next-door neighbor/the students in the class next door/the principal of the school/a famous movie or TV star/a famous sports celebrity?

A sparkling camp

It's Friday afternoon in June at the Tukabatchee Summer Camp. The camp counselors are supposed to be working, but they aren't. The camp has to be ready for the first summer campers. They'll arrive tomorrow. The counselors have had lunch, and they're taking it easy in the counselors' lounge. Their camp director has just opened the door. He's brought the duty roster with him, so he knows exactly what each of them should be doing.

Director: Hey, what's going on here?

Exercise 1

Look at Terri in the picture. Ask and answer about the other counselors.

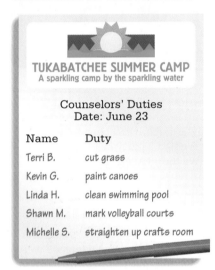

TUKABATCHEE SUMMER CAMP
A sparkling camp by the sparkling water

**Counselors' Duties
Date: June 23**

Name	Duty
Terri B.	cut grass
Kevin G.	paint canoes
Linda H.	clean swimming pool
Shawn M.	mark volleyball courts
Michelle S.	straighten up crafts room

1. *What's she doing?*
   She's lying on the sofa.
   She's drinking iced tea.
   She's watching TV.

2. *Should she be watching TV?*
   No, she shouldn't.
   Should she be cutting the grass?
   Yes, she should.

3. *What should she be doing?*
   She should be cutting the grass.
   What shouldn't she be doing?
   She shouldn't be lying on the sofa.
   She shouldn't be drinking iced tea.
   She shouldn't be watching TV.

Director: Terri! What are you doing?
Terri: I'm watching TV.
Director: And what are you supposed to be doing?
Terri: I'm not sure.
Director: Well, let me tell you, Terri. You're supposed to be cutting the grass.
Terri: Oh, right. I'm sorry. I'll get right on it.
Director: When I come back, you'd better be cutting the grass. Do you hear me?
Terri: OK, OK. I'm going.
Director: Get a move on, Terri. Remember the Tukabatchee motto: "A sparkling camp by the sparkling water."

Exercise 2

Make similar conversations between the director and the other counselors.

Look at this:

Exercise 3

Terri is cutting the grass.
She'd rather not be cutting the grass.
She'd rather be lying on the beach.

Write sentences about the other counselors.

Exercise 4

What are you doing?
What would you rather be doing?

Write five sentences.

A funny thing happened to me last Friday. I'd gone into New York to do some holiday shopping. I wanted to get some presents, and I wanted to see the city all decorated for the holidays—you know, the store windows and the big tree at Rockefeller Center. I had gotten into the city early, so by early afternoon I'd bought everything I wanted. Anyway, I was really tired—all that shopping in crowded stores—and I'd made plans for that night. I just wanted to get home so I could relax before I had to go out again. I went to the Long Island Railroad at Penn Station. It was well before rush hour. I had apparently just missed a train, and the next one wouldn't be leaving for 40 minutes, so I decided I had time for a cup of coffee. I bought a *Times* and went into a small doughnut shop and sat at the counter. I ordered a cup of coffee and a box of a half-dozen assorted mini-doughnuts—I figured I would eat a couple and take the rest home for my family. Anyway, they were having a special on the mini-doughnuts, and I can't resist a bargain. I started the crossword puzzle in the paper.

A few minutes later a woman sat down next to me on the stool to my left. That surprised me because there were several empty stools. There was nothing strange about her except that she was very tall. In fact, she looked like a typical businesswoman—you know, conservative suit, briefcase. I didn't say anything; I just kept doing the crossword. Suddenly she reached out, opened the box of doughnuts, took one out, dunked it in her coffee, and began to eat it. I couldn't believe my eyes! Anyway, I didn't want to make a scene, so I decided to ignore it. I always avoid trouble if I can. I just took a doughnut myself and went back to my crossword.

When the woman took a second doughnut I didn't say a word. After all, if I hadn't protested when she took the first one, how could I say anything when she took the second one? I pretended to be very interested in the puzzle. A few minutes later I casually put out my hand, took another doughnut, and glanced at the woman. She seemed to be glaring at me. She was making me feel so nervous that I decided to have a third doughnut. That left only one—for only a minute. Sure enough, the woman took the last doughnut! I

nervously continued eating my doughnut and decided to leave. I was ready to get up and go when the woman suddenly stood up and hurried out of the doughnut shop. I felt very relieved and decided to wait for two or three minutes before going myself. I finished my second cup of coffee, folded my newspaper, and stood up. And there, on the counter, underneath where my paper had been, was my unopened box of doughnuts.

Exercise 1

Find words or expressions that mean:
1. evidently *apparently*
2. looked briefly *glanced*
3. stay away from *avoid*
4. acted as if I was *pretended*
5. unwind *relax*
6. thought *figured*
7. coolly *casually*
8. say no to *protest*
9. traditional *conservative*
10. a buy *bargain*

Exercise 2

Discuss: Has anything like this ever happened to you? Have you ever, by mistake, taken anything that didn't belong to you?

Part 1

Charles Beresford Tifton was found dead on the floor of his study in the Tifton family mansion in New Orleans. He had been shot five times. There were five people on the estate, and they all heard the shots at about 4:00 PM. The police have taken statements and made the following notes about each of the five people.

Lydia Dubois Tifton, 62
Married to Charles Tifton for 35 years. Has been in a wheelchair since a riding accident 12 years ago. Had a loud argument with Ruth Ellen Potts this morning. Told Tifton to fire Ruth Ellen. After long argument, Tifton refused.

LYDIA TIFTON'S STATEMENT

I was reading in my bedroom on the first floor. I heard the shots; there were four or five. I wheeled myself into the hall. The study door was open. Ruth Ellen was standing in the doorway screaming. Benson was standing at the French windows. The gun was on the floor next to my husband's body.

J.D. Tifton, 33
Tifton's only child. Reputation as a gambler and a playboy. Thrown out of three colleges. Has large gambling debts. Arrested last year for drug possession. Given suspended sentence. His father had refused to let him have any more money. Heir to the Tifton fortune. Will inherit $50,000,000.

J.D.'S STATEMENT

I was in the den. I was listening to a new CD. Suddenly there were five shots. I thought it was Uncle Ike at target practice. Then I heard a scream. It sounded like Ruth Ellen, so I opened the connecting door to the study and saw Big Daddy lying there, Benson at the French windows, and Mama and Ruth Ellen together in the doorway to the hall. I couldn't believe my eyes.

🎧 Listening

Listen to Dwight's statement to the police. Where does he say he was? What does he claim he was doing?

Ruth Ellen Potts, 24
Has been Tifton's private secretary for a year. Had recently been seen with J.D. Tifton at a new club, The Red Parrot, near the French Quarter. The senior Tifton was very upset about it. Threatened to fire her but didn't.

RUTH ELLEN POTTS'S STATEMENT

I was in the living room writing my résumé. I heard the shots and ran across the hall. The door to the study was open. There was poor, dear Charles—Mr. Tifton—lying in a pool of blood. I started screaming. Benson came in through the French windows; they were open. Then Mrs. Tifton arrived. She didn't say a word. She just stared at me.

Harold Benson, 65
Butler. Has been with the Tifton family for nearly 40 years. Will retire in two months. Likes good wine and good food. Takes Lydia Tifton out every day in her wheelchair. Knows everything about the family. Knows Ruth Ellen's mother very well. Introduced Ruth Ellen to the Tiftons. Had long argument with the victim in the morning.

BENSON'S STATEMENT

I was about to take my afternoon walk. The doctor told me to walk twice a day for my heart. Anyway, I had just come out of the back door, and I was walking around the corner of the house when I heard shooting. I ran across the lawn to the French windows. I saw Mr. Charles's body and Miss Ruth Ellen in the doorway.

Dwight ("Ike") Dubois, 60
Lydia Tifton's brother. Was Olympic rifle-shooting champion. Doesn't work—spends time hunting and fishing. Was chief executive officer of Pontchartrain Land Development Corporation, one of Tifton's companies. Went to prison for two years when the company collapsed with debts of over $2 million after a big land scandal. Has lived on the Tifton estate since getting out of prison.

Part 2

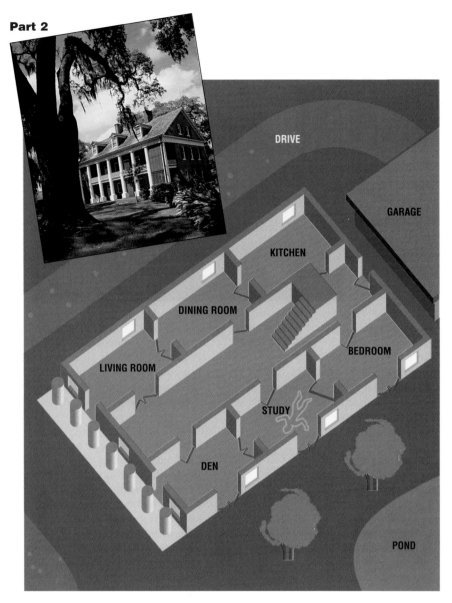

Labels on floor plan: DRIVE, GARAGE, KITCHEN, DINING ROOM, BEDROOM, LIVING ROOM, STUDY, DEN, POND

Novak: But he was over 60! He was old enough to be Potts's grandfather.
Damato: Hmm…yes, but he was a good-looking man—and very rich and powerful.

DWIGHT DUBOIS?

Damato: What about Dubois, Novak? He's a weird guy.
Novak: I've been thinking about that. It couldn't have been him.
Damato: Why not?
Novak: Why would he need to shoot five times? He was a champion marksman. He could have killed him with one shot.
Damato: Maybe he did, Novak, maybe he did.
Novak: I don't follow.
Damato: There are a lot of things you don't follow, Novak. Maybe he's smarter than he looks.
Novak: But there's no motive.
Damato: There might have been. I mean there was the scandal with that land development company.
Novak: But he was down by the pond.
Damato: So? He could have shot him from the trees and thrown the gun into the room.
Novak: Oh, yeah. Do you really think so?
Damato: I don't know. It's just a theory.

Chief of Detectives Tony Damato is in charge of the case. Detective Sergeant Novak is his assistant. They're in the Tifton study.

Damato: Where is everybody?
Novak: They're all in the living room. Reyes is with them. What do you think?
Damato: It could have been any of them, couldn't it? Nobody seems very sad. It might even have been all of them.
Novak: Yeah. Tifton wasn't exactly popular around here. Nobody liked him. But it could have been an outsider.
Damato: No way. It must have been one of them. Let's look at the evidence.
Novak: It seems to me that everybody has a motive, and

nobody has an alibi. They all say they were alone when it happened.
Damato: Yes, and there are no fingerprints on the gun.

LYDIA TIFTON?

Novak: It couldn't have been her.
Damato: Why not?
Novak: Well, she's in a wheelchair. She can't move very fast. Anyway, they've been married for 35 years. It just couldn't have been her.
Damato: Most murders are committed by someone in the family, and that door goes into her room.
Novak: Right, but it was locked.
Damato: Doors have keys.
Novak: But why would she want to kill him?
Damato: Ruth Ellen Potts is a very attractive young woman. We don't know what was going on. She might have been jealous.

Look at this:

Could	it have been	him? her? them?

It	must could(n't) may (not) might (not)	have been	him. her. them.

Could	he she they	have	shot him? killed him? been the one(s)?

He She They	must could(n't) may (not) might (not)	have	shot him. killed him. been the one.

Exercise

Discuss each character. Make a list of sentences about all five suspects. Who do you think did it? How? Why?

Good evening. I'm Harry Baxter and this is *Call-In* on radio station WLFM. We're talking tonight about government services. Do you think you're getting what you've paid for? What's your opinion? Call in. We'd like to hear from you. The number is 555-1785.

Call-In. You're on the air.

Stuart: Hi, Harry. My name is Stuart Amos. I'm a salesman and I have to drive a lot. Why is it that there's always construction going on on all the alternate routes at exactly the same time? I mean, I understand that the roads need to be maintained, but there's absolutely no coordination. Like, when they're fixing one bridge into the city, why do they have to fix the other bridge at the same time? It's ridiculous!

Harry: Good point, Stuart. Let's hope the Department of Transportation folks are listening! Call-In. You're on the air.

Hilda: Good evening, Harry. I'm Hilda Diaz. Why are they closing the fire station in my neighborhood? We need it to stay open. I heard that the, uh, response time is going to be increased by ten minutes if that fire station closes. Ten minutes! That could mean the difference between life and death, you know. If they're trying to save money, why don't those politicians all take a pay cut? That's where the waste is, if you ask me!

Harry: Well, Hilda, you certainly sound passionate. We'll see if the city doesn't change its mind. I hope you've called your city council representative. Call-In. You're on the air.

Milton: Harry, I'm Milton Kramer. I'm fed up with those sanitation trucks that come in the middle of the night and make all that noise. They must start at around four o'clock in the morning! And it's every other night. I'm sound asleep and I have about three more hours before the alarm's going to go off, and the garbage truck comes. I can never get back to sleep, and before I know it, I have to get up for work. It ruins my whole day. There must be a way for them to change the schedule so they don't wake up the neighborhood.

Harry: You know, Milton, I've never understood why sanitation trucks have to come in the middle of the night, either. I'm sure the sanitation workers wouldn't mind having different hours, say, like seven o'clock to four o'clock. And on that note, it's time to say good night. Thank you for listening, and remember to tune in again tomorrow.

Exercise

Discuss: What improvements do you think your city/town government should make?

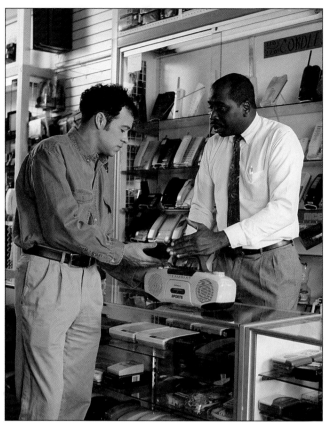

Customer: Good morning. I'd like to speak to the manager.

Manager: I am the manager, sir. How can I help you?

Customer: Well, it's this radio. It doesn't work.

Manager: Hmm…did you buy it here?

Customer: What? Of course I bought it here. Look, you turn it on and nothing happens.

Manager: May I see your receipt?

Customer: Receipt? Uh…I don't have one.

Manager: You must have gotten a receipt when you bought it.

Customer: I probably did. I must have thrown it away.

Manager: Uh-huh. Well, do you have any other proof of purchase—the guarantee, for example?

Customer: No. It must have been in the box. I threw that away too.

Manager: That's too bad. You really ought to have kept it. We need to know the exact date of purchase.

Customer: What? I only bought it yesterday! That young man over there waited on me…. Oh, I paid by credit card. I have my copy here.

Manager: Oh. All right then. Did you test the radio before you left the store?

Customer: Test it? No, it was in the original box. I expected it to work. It wasn't some cheap radio; it's a good brand.

Manager: You should have tested it.

Customer: Come on! Stop telling me what I should have done, and do something! Either give me my money back or give me another radio.

Manager: There's no need to get impatient, sir. Let me look at it. Hmm…you see this little switch in the back?

Customer: Yes.

Manager: It's on AC and it should be on DC. You really should have read the instructions.

Customer: Oh!

Look at this:

> 174 Logan Drive
> San Diego, CA 92013
> May 22, 1995
>
> Customer Service Dept.
> Peers Lowbruck Co.
> Chicago, IL 60606
>
> Dear Sir or Madam:
>
> Last week I bought a pocket calculator at your store in Anaheim, California. It seemed to work in the store. When I got home, I discovered it was defective. It performs arithmetic functions fine, but the memory function does not work at all. I took it back to your store in San Diego, but they refused to exchange it. They said that I would have to return it to the store where I bought it. This is impossible because I do not live in Anaheim.
>
> I have enclosed the calculator along with the receipt, showing the price and date of purchase, and your guarantee. I would appreciate a full refund.
>
> Thank you. If you have any questions, please call me at (619) 235-6596.
>
> Sincerely,
>
> *Gail Yamamura*
> Gail Yamamura
>
> Enclosure

Exercise

> ### One-Year Warranty
> **Digital Alarm Clock**
> **model K9-12-B**
> This clock has been inspected and tested in our factory and was shipped in perfect working order. If it fails to perform perfectly under normal conditions within twelve (12) months of your purchase, return it to us in the original package, enclosing a copy of your receipt. We will repair it or replace it with a new one, free of charge.
>
> QUARTZ KLOX
> P.O. Box 307
> Fair Oaks, CA 95628

You bought a digital alarm clock at a Valuworth store on Main Street in your town last week. It said *blue* on the box, but the clock was pink. The alarm doesn't seem to work. You paid cash, and you didn't keep the receipt.

Look at the owner's warranty. Write a letter of complaint to the Quartz Klox company.

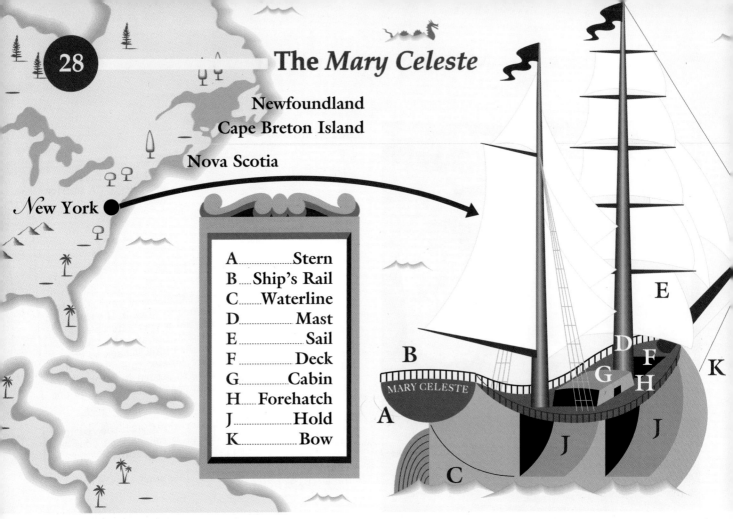

The *Mary Celeste*

Newfoundland
Cape Breton Island
Nova Scotia

New York

A................Stern
B.....Ship's Rail
C........Waterline
D................Mast
E....................Sail
F..................Deck
G.................Cabin
H.....Forehatch
J....................Hold
K....................Bow

MARY CELESTE

The *Mary Celeste* was built in 1861 in Nova Scotia, Canada, as a cargo-carrying sailing ship. When it was launched, it was given the name *Amazon*. It was not a lucky ship. The first captain died a few days after it was registered, and on its first voyage, in 1862, it was badly damaged in a collision. While it was being repaired in port, it caught fire. In 1863, it crossed the Atlantic for the first time, and in the English Channel it collided with another ship that sank. The *Amazon* was badly damaged itself. In 1867, it ran aground on Cape Breton Island, off the Canadian coast, and had to be rebuilt. It was then sold and the name was changed to the *Mary Celeste*. Sailors are very superstitious and dislike sailing on ships which have been unlucky or which have changed their names. Many sailors refused to sail on the *Mary Celeste*.

On November 5, 1872, the *Mary Celeste* left New York, carrying a cargo of industrial alcohol to Genoa in Italy. There were eleven people on board: Captain Briggs, an experienced captain, his wife and two-year-old daughter, and a crew of eight.

A month later, the *Mary Celeste* was seen by another ship, the *Dei Gratia*, about halfway between the Azores and the Portuguese coast. Captain

Moorhouse of the *Dei Gratia*, a friend of Captain Briggs, noticed that the ship was sailing strangely. When the *Mary Celeste* did not answer his signal, he sent a small boat to find out what was wrong.

The *Mary Celeste* was completely deserted.
• The only lifeboat was missing.
• All the sails were up and in good condition.
• All the cargo was there.
• The ship had obviously been through storms. The glass cover on the compass was broken.
• The windows of the deck cabins had been covered with wooden planks.
• There was three feet of water in the cargo hold, which was not enough to be dangerous.
• The water pumps were working perfectly.
• There was enough food for six months and plenty of fresh water.
• All the crew's personal possessions (clothes, boots, pipes and tobacco, etc.) were on board.
• There were toys on the captain's bed.
• There was food and drink on the cabin table.
• Only the navigation instruments and ship's papers were missing.
• The last entry in the ship's logbook had been made 11 days earlier,

about 600 miles west, but the ship had continued in a straight line from there.
• The forehatch was found open.
• There were two deep marks on the bow, near the waterline.
• There was a deep cut on the ship's rail, made by an axe.
• There were old brown bloodstains on the deck and on the captain's sword, which was in the cabin.

Captain Moorhouse and his crew were given the salvage money for bringing the ship to port. There was a long official investigation, but the story of what happened on the ship, and what happened to the crew, still remains a mystery.

Exercise

Find words that mean:
1. all the people working on a ship
2. the official daily written record of a ship's voyage
3. the front of a ship
4. put a boat into the water
5. an instrument that shows the position of "north"
6. a weapon
7. a long, thin, narrow, flat piece of wood
8. payment given to those who save other's property at sea
9. goods carried on a ship
10. a machine for forcing water into or out of something

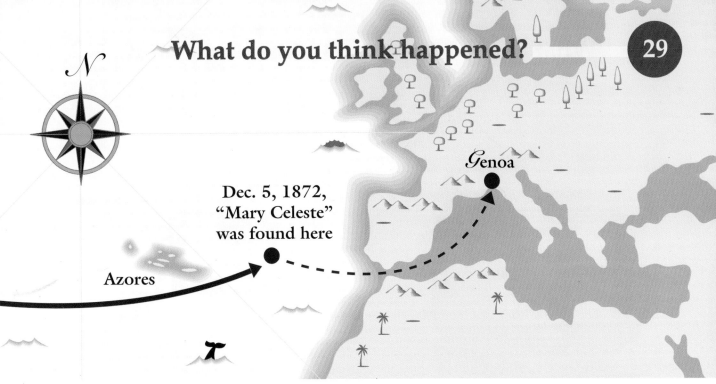

Dec. 5, 1872, "Mary Celeste" was found here

Azores

Genoa

Sarah: I don't know what happened, but it must have happened suddenly.

Mark: Why do you think that?

Sarah: Think about it. There were toys on the captain's bed, weren't there? The kid must have been playing, and they must have interrupted her suddenly.

Mark: Yes, that's true. And food was on the table. They must have been eating or getting ready to eat.

Sarah: The lifeboat was missing, right? They could have been practicing their emergency drill. They must have gotten into the boat and launched it.

Mark: All right, but what happened to the boat?

Sarah: Well, they may have been rowing the lifeboat around the ship, and there must have been a gust of wind; then the ship could have moved forward and run down the lifeboat. That explains the marks on the bow.

Mark: Come on. They couldn't have all been sitting in the lifeboat. What about the captain? He should have been steering the ship!

Sarah: Well, he might have been watching the drill and jumped in to save the others.

Amazingly, all of these possible explanations of what happened have been suggested at some time:

THE CREW ABANDONED THE SHIP.

1. There was water in the hold. The crew panicked and abandoned the ship because they thought it was going to sink.

2. The girl fell overboard. The mother jumped in to save her. They launched a lifeboat to rescue her.

3. One of the barrels of alcohol was damaged. Perhaps there was a small explosion. The hatch cover was off, either because of the explosion or to let the gas escape. They thought all of the cargo might explode.

4. The last log entry was 1,000 kilometers (600 miles) west, near Santa Maria Island. Maybe the ship was in danger of running aground on the island. The crew left the ship in a storm.

5. There was no wind, so they got into the lifeboat to tow the ship. The rope broke.

6. They saw an island that was not on the map and went to investigate.

7. A member of the crew had a terrible, infectious disease. The others left to escape from it. The one with the disease killed himself.

WHAT ABOUT THE LIFEBOAT?

If the crew left the ship by lifeboat, what happened to them?

1. The lifeboat could have sunk in a storm.

2. The ship itself could have run down the lifeboat.

3. The lifeboat could have drifted away, and all of them could have died of hunger and thirst.

4. They might have reached land. They were robbed and killed there.

5. A whale or sharks might have overturned the boat.

A CRIME WAS COMMITTED.

1. The *Dei Gratia* attacked the *Mary Celeste* and killed everybody.

2. Pirates attacked and killed them.

3. There was a mutiny (a revolt against the captain of a ship). Two of the members of the crew were criminals. There was a fight. Some were killed. The others left.

4. Mrs. Briggs fell in love with a crew member. Again, there was a fight.

5. The crew of the *Mary Celeste* attacked and robbed another ship and left on the other ship with its cargo. (What other ship? There are no records.)

6. They found an abandoned ship with a valuable cargo and stole it.

7. Captain Briggs and Captain Moorhouse planned everything together for the salvage money. The ship was never abandoned. None of the story was true.

OUTSIDE FORCES WERE AT PLAY.

1. A UFO (unidentified flying object) took everybody away.

2. A giant wave or a tornado knocked them all from the deck.

3. A sea monster (a giant octopus or sea serpent) attacked the ship.

4. Men living below the sea attacked the ship when it passed over the old site of Atlantis.

Exercise

Choose one group of explanations and discuss whether or not they make sense.

1. Marilyn Monroe was born Norma Jean Mortenson in Los Angeles on June 1, 1926. Norma Jean never knew her father. Her mother, whose maiden name was Monroe, was mentally ill and was often confined to mental institutions. As a result, Norma Jean lived with her mother's friends, in an orphanage, and with various foster parents, where she was often neglected and abused.

2. At the age of 16, Norma Jean left high school and married Jim Dougherty, who was 21. Their marriage wasn't very happy. Two years later, Dougherty, a merchant marine, went overseas, and Norma Jean began working as a paint sprayer in a defense plant. It was there that she was "discovered" by a U.S. Army photographer, who asked her to pose for some photographs for a magazine article. She was soon noticed by other photographers and encouraged to enter a modeling agency, where her brown hair was bleached and restyled. It was now 1946. That year, she divorced Dougherty, who was still overseas. Later that year, she signed a one-year contract with Twentieth-Century Fox Studios, and her name was changed to Marilyn Monroe.

3. In the years between 1946 and 1950, Marilyn got only small parts. But by 1953, she had starred in two of her most famous comedies, *Gentlemen Prefer Blondes* and *How to Marry a Millionaire*. In January 1954, Marilyn

married baseball hero Joe DiMaggio. She was then Twentieth-Century Fox's biggest box-office attraction and an international sex goddess. Only nine months after they got married, while she was working on *The Seven Year Itch*, Marilyn and DiMaggio got divorced, but they remained friends for the rest of her life.

4. In 1955, Marilyn announced the formation of Marilyn Monroe Productions. She wanted to play serious roles instead of the "dumb blonde" roles she usually got. She began taking acting classes at the famous Actors Studio, and associating with New York's intellectual crowd. It was then that she met the playwright Arthur Miller. In December 1955, Twentieth-Century Fox got her to sign another contract, promising her more serious roles and approval over her films' directors. Her first film under the new contract was the drama *Bus Stop*, for which she won critical acclaim.

5. In June 1956, Marilyn and Arthur Miller were married. She then starred in three comedies: *The Prince and the Showgirl* (1957), the smash hit *Some Like It Hot* (1959), and *Let's Make Love* (1960). Marilyn then starred in the drama *The Misfits*, which was written especially for her by her playwright husband. During the filming, Marilyn was frequently ill and depressed, and she became dependent on sleeping pills, tranquilizers, and alcohol. She saw a psychiatrist every day. In

January 1961, a week before the opening of *The Misfits*, she divorced Miller. About a month later, she was hospitalized. She was seriously ill, both physically and emotionally.

6. In May 1962, Marilyn again became emotionally distressed and physically ill, and the filming of her newest movie, *Something's Got to Give*, was delayed. In early June, Twentieth-Century Fox fired Marilyn from the movie and began a negative publicity campaign, labeling her mentally ill. Marilyn then entered a Hollywood hospital for three days under an assumed name. There were rumors that she was (or had been) pregnant. When she got out of the hospital, she re-negotiated with Twentieth-Century Fox and planned to return to work on *Something's Got to Give*.

7. In the last week before her death, Marilyn had three business meetings, selected dozens of plants for her garden, appeared on the cover of *Life* Magazine, ordered a $10,000 evening gown, and spent more than ten hours with her psychiatrist.

8. On August 4, Marilyn called her psychiatrist, who went to her home and held a 90-minute session with her that probably involved an injection of barbiturates. After her psychiatrist left, Marilyn spoke to friends and others, none of whom thought she was acting unusual. That night, at

10:30 PM, Marilyn's housekeeper discovered her body. She called Marilyn's psychiatrist.

9. On August 5, 1962, at 4:25 AM, Marilyn's psychiatrist called the Los Angeles police and reported, "Marilyn Monroe is dead. She just committed suicide." Police Sergeant Jack Clemmons arrived on the scene and believed the suicide had been staged. He told the press on Sunday, "Marilyn Monroe didn't commit suicide; she was murdered."

Exercise

Find another way to say each expression highlighted below.

1. Marilyn was often seen *spending time* with New York's intellectual crowd.
2. She was given *the right to accept or reject* her directors.
3. Her first husband spent several years *abroad*.
4. She was emotionally *upset* and physically ill.
5. She became *addicted* to sleeping pills and alcohol.
6. The filming of the movie was *held up*.
7. Her performance received *high praise from the critics*.
8. The movie studio fired her, *calling her mentally ill*.
9. As a child, she was often *ignored* by her foster parents.
10. The psychiatrist probably gave her *a shot* of barbiturates.

How did Marilyn Monroe die? Here are some popular theories.

It was suicide.
(This is the official cause of death given by the Los Angeles County Coroner.)

It was murder.

It was an accident.
Marilyn's death was the result of a terrible accident caused by the interaction of two drugs given to her by separate physicians.

A: Hello?
B: Hi, Rafael. This is Alex.
A: Oh, hi. Did you get home all right?
B: Yeah, thanks, but I wanted to apologize for last night.
A: Don't worry about it.
B: But your carpet! It must be ruined. It was so dumb of me to put my coffee on the floor.
A: Come on, Alex, forget it.
B: But it must have made a really ugly stain.
A: Look, it's nothing. I was upset at first, but it doesn't look so bad this morning.
B: Anyway, I want to pay for the cleaning.
A: Listen, Alex, it's no big deal. Accidents happen—at parties especially.
B: Well, if you say so, but I really am sorry.
A: OK. See you on Monday. Bye now.

E: Oh! Good morning, Mary Ann.
F: Good afternoon, Sharon. Late again, I see.
E: *(Sigh)* Yes. I'm sorry. I couldn't find a parking space.
F: Maybe you should have left home earlier.
E: Yes, I know. It won't happen again, Mary Ann.
F: It'd better not, Sharon. This is the third time this week.

I: Are you all right?
J: Yes, I'm OK, but what about my car?
I: There doesn't seem to be too much damage.
J: Let me see…look at that! This is a brand-new car! You shouldn't have been going so fast.
I: Well, it wasn't my fault.
J: It wasn't your fault?! What do you mean, it wasn't your fault? I had the right of way.
I: As a matter of fact, you didn't. You shouldn't have come out like that.
J: Why not? There's no sign.
I: Then what's that?
J: Oh. A stop sign. I must have missed it.
I: Well, you should have been more careful. You could have gotten us all killed.
J: Yes, you're right. I'm sorry. What else can I say?
I: Just thank goodness nobody's hurt. Here come the police. You'd better explain it to them.

C: Excuse me. Would you mind not walking on the grass?
D: I beg your pardon?
C: You aren't allowed to walk on the grass.
D: Really? I didn't see a sign.
C: There it is. Right over there.
D: Oh, you're right. I'm terribly sorry.

G: Hey, you!
H: Are you talking to me?
G: Yeah, you. What do you think you're doing?
H: I'm just waiting for the bus.
G: Can't you see there's a line?
H: Oh, there is? I'm sorry. I didn't mean to cut. I didn't realize there was a line.

TRUCK HIJACKED IN BEDFORD

$200,000 CARGO STOLEN

A truck carrying television sets, video recorders, radios, and other electronics valued at over $200,000 was hijacked yesterday morning. The truck belonged to the Ruby Star Company, and the driver, Nicolas Estrella, was making deliveries to the customers in the Bedford section.

This is the eleventh truck hijacking in the first five months of this year. Over the last four years there have been 38 hijackings in the metropolitan area. The hijackers concentrate on trucks carrying cargoes that can be sold quickly for cash.

Drivers have been warned to lock their doors and not pick up hitchhikers. But some insurance investigators believe that as many as one-third of these cases are not hijackings at all. They believe that dishonest drivers steal their own cargoes.

(continued on page B6)

Police Captain Mel Torino is questioning Nicolas Estrella, the driver of the hijacked Ruby Star truck.

Captain: Let's start at the beginning again, Mr. Estrella. How did you lose your truck?

Mr. Estrella: I was making deliveries in Bedford. The truck was loaded with TVs, VCRs, radios…you know, electronics.

Captain: Uh-huh. So you drove to Bedford from the Ruby Star warehouse.

Mr. Estrella: Right. About ten o'clock I made a delivery on Boyle Street. I'd finished and I was driving up Boyle when I saw a coffee shop.

Captain: So you decided to stop.

Mr. Estrella: That's right. I stopped to get a sandwich to go.

Captain: Go on.

Mr. Estrella: It didn't take me more than three minutes. I started walking back to the truck and…

Captain: Did you see anybody near the truck?

Mr. Estrella: No, nobody. So anyway, I decided to make a phone call. I passed a magazine stand and I stopped to get change.

Captain: OK. Then what?

Mr. Estrella: Well, I was talking to my wife when I saw the truck going down the street. I couldn't believe my eyes. I dropped the phone and ran down the street. But they were moving fast. I couldn't catch up.

Captain: Did you remember to lock the cab door?

Mr. Estrella: Yes, I always remember to lock it! I'm not stupid!

Captain: OK, OK, take it easy. Can you actually remember locking it this time?

Mr. Estrella: Yes, definitely. I remember putting the key in the lock. The key was all wet and dirty. It was raining, and I had dropped it in a puddle.

Captain: What about the door on the other side? Did you remember to check it?

Mr. Estrella: I don't actually remember checking it. But it's always locked, and I never use it.

Captain: But you don't remember checking it?

Mr. Estrella: No, not really. Maybe I forgot to check it.

Captain: So it could have been open.

Mr. Estrella: Yes, I guess so. But I'd bet anything it wasn't.

Captain: So what's your theory?

Mr. Estrella: They must have had keys. They started the engine, didn't they?

Captain: How did they get the keys?

Mr. Estrella: Don't ask me. I have no idea. They didn't stop to tell me!

Look at this:

He was driving. He stopped. He got a sandwich.
A: *What did he stop doing? He stopped driving.*
B: *What did he stop to do? He stopped to get a sandwich.*

Exercise 1

Ask two questions and give answers for each.
1. He was driving. He stopped. He bought some gas.
2. He was watching the truck. He stopped. He made a phone call.
3. He was talking to his wife. He stopped. He ran down the street.

Look at this:

I drove a car for the first time when I was 16. I was so nervous but so happy that day!
I remember driving a car for the first time.

I was going to mail this letter. I still have it.
I didn't remember to mail it.
I forgot to mail it.

Exercise 2

Make sentences.
1. I should have turned off the light. It's still on.
2. I read about the crime in the newspaper. I can remember it clearly.
3. There's a movie on TV tonight. I saw it at a theater ten years ago.
4. They ought to have done their homework. Their teacher's very upset.

John Lennon was murdered just before 11 PM on December 8, 1980, outside the Dakota, the apartment building where he lived in New York City. He had just gotten out of a car and was walking to the entrance when a voice called, "Mr. Lennon." Lennon turned and was shot five times. The killer threw his gun down and stood there smiling. "Do you know what you just did?" shouted the doorman. "I just shot John Lennon," the killer replied. Lennon was rushed to the hospital in a police car, but it was too late. The killer was 25-year-old Mark Chapman from Hawaii. Earlier the same evening he had asked Lennon for his autograph. In fact, he had been hanging around outside the apartment building for several days. Chapman was a fan of Lennon's and had tried to imitate him in many ways. It is said that he even believed that he **was** John Lennon.

BIOGRAPHICAL NOTES

1940   Born in Liverpool, England.
1942   Lennon family deserted by father. Mother leaves. John brought up by aunt.
1956   Forms rock band at school.
1957   Student at Liverpool College of Art.
1958   Mother killed in car accident.
1960   Goes professional as one of the Beatles (Lennon, McCartney, Harrison, Best, Sutcliffe). Plays in Hamburg, Germany.
1961   Plays in Hamburg and Liverpool. Sutcliffe (Lennon's best friend) dies of brain tumor. Brian Epstein begins to manage the Beatles.
1962   Ringo Starr replaces Pete Best as Beatles' drummer. Marries Cynthia Powell, an art student. Beatles' first record, "Love Me Do." First TV appearance.

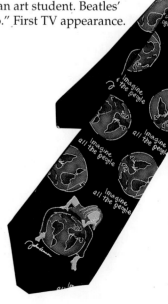

1963 Three records hit number 1 in British Top 20. Incredible popularity. Son Julian born.

1964 First hit record in United States, "I Want to Hold Your Hand." Two U.S. tours. In April, Beatles' records number 1, 2, 3, 4, and 5 in U.S. Top 40. First movie, *A Hard Day's Night.* First book.

1965 *Help!* Beatles' second movie. Beatlemania at its height. U.S. tour. Huge audiences in sports stadiums. Beatles receive MBE (special honorary award) from Queen Elizabeth.

1966 Lennon in movie *How I Won the War*—not a musical. Meets Yoko Ono, Japanese avant-garde artist.

1967 *Sergeant Pepper*—Beatles' most famous album. All the Beatles interested in meditation. Manager Brian Epstein found dead from overdose of sleeping pills.

1968 Beatles' company, Apple, founded. Lennon art exhibit "You Are Here." Lennon divorced by wife.

1969 Beatles' movie *Let It Be.* Rumors of quarrels about money. Talk of Beatles breaking up. Beatles' last public performance on roof of Apple Building. Lennon and Yoko marry. He 29, she 36. Lennon still recording with Beatles but also works solo.

1970 McCartney leaves Beatles. Others start solo careers.

1971 Lennon's album *Imagine*—most successful solo album. Lennon and Yoko Ono in New York one-room studio apartment.

1973 Lennon ordered to leave United States—protests and appeals.

1975 Son Sean born October 9 (Lennon's birthday).

1976 Retires from public life. Extensive travel. Business affairs managed by Yoko Ono.

1980 First record in six years. Album *Double Fantasy.* Critics say it is "a new beginning." Dec. 8, Lennon murdered. Massive media coverage.

1981 Three records in Top 40: "(Just Like) Starting Over," "Imagine," and "Woman."

1985 "Strawberry Fields" memorial to Lennon opens in New York's Central Park on October 9, Sean Lennon's tenth birthday.

1988 Beatles inducted into Rock 'n' Roll Hall of Fame.

1990 Tribute concert to Lennon in Liverpool featuring McCartney.

1994 Lennon inducted into the Rock 'n' Roll Hall of Fame as solo artist. Three surviving Beatles add their voices and instruments to an old Lennon tape, "Free As a Bird"—the final Beatles recording.

Exercise 1

Look at this:

<u>Unless</u> he turns around soon, he'll be in trouble.

If he doesn't turn around soon, he'll be in trouble.

Find all the sentences with *unless* and make sentences with *if … not.*

Exercise 2

If you were the man who almost drowned, would you give the lifeguards a reward? What else would you do?

If you were the man who almost drowned, would you do anything differently in the future? What would you do?

Exercise 3

What would you do in these emergencies? Discuss.

You see someone fall into a river. You're alone.

You're at a restaurant with a friend and your friend starts choking.

You're walking down a street and you see smoke coming out of a house.

Mike: Wanda, have you seen this ad?

Wanda: Yeah. It looks great, doesn't it? I called them an hour ago. They'll call back if they want me.

Mike: Oh, they'll want you. You have beautiful hair.

Wanda: Thanks. You know, I'm excited. I mean, if I go, I'll get a new hairstyle for nothing!

Louis: Pablo, look at this. It sounds great. And you have a decent car…

Pablo: Uh-huh. But there are some disadvantages.

Louis: Every job has disadvantages.

Pablo: Oh, I don't know. I'm willing to try it. But I won't take it if they don't pay the phone bill!

Roger: Tina, what do you think of this ad?

Tina: It was in last Sunday's paper too. I called. I have an interview tomorrow.

Roger: Do you think you'll get it?

Tina: They seemed very interested on the phone. I think they'll offer me the job.

Roger: So you're going to France!

Tina: I didn't say that. I won't take the job unless they give me a round-trip ticket. It'll be hard work, and I won't go unless they offer me a good salary.

Sandy: Hey, Bill, look at this ad.

Bill: Hmm…it looks like fun. Why don't you call them up?

Sandy: I'd love to, but it's a waste of time. My hair's just too short.

Bill: Well, I like it the way it is. Anyway, you don't know what they might do…

Sandy: Oh, that wouldn't bother me. If I had longer hair, I'd call them up. Actually, **your** hair is pretty long now…

Kathy: Pam, did you see this?

Pam: Yeah. You aren't interested, are you?

Kathy: No, there are too many things wrong with it.

Pam: Like what?

Kathy: Are you kidding? You wouldn't have any security. You wouldn't earn anything if you didn't work all day long every day. And I wouldn't take a job in sales if they didn't provide a car.

Pam: Look at the address—some hotel. I'd never work for a company if they didn't even have an office.

Kitty: There's a job in France in the paper.

Terry: Yeah, I know. I wouldn't dream of taking it.

Kitty: Why not? You've always wanted to work overseas.

Terry: It's hard work, isn't it? One night off a week.

Kitty: But the money might be good.

Terry: Well, I wouldn't take it unless they paid me a really good salary, with a longer vacation, and more free time. And I certainly wouldn't go anywhere overseas unless my ticket was round-trip!

Look at this:

I'm interested. I've applied.

I'll accept the job if they offer enough money.

I won't accept the job if they don't pay more.

I won't accept the job unless they pay more.

I'm not interested. I haven't applied.

I'd apply if they offered more money.

I wouldn't accept the job if they didn't offer enough.

I wouldn't accept the job unless they offered more.

Exercise

Would you ever travel alone to a foreign country?
Not unless I knew someone there.
I wouldn't travel alone to a foreign country unless I knew someone there.
Would you ever: hit someone/jump from a high building/take your clothes off in the street/jump off a moving train/walk on hot coals/go skydiving/make a speech in English/sing in front of an audience?

Farther = DISTance ⊘
Further – No DISTance.

Glacier watch

Alaska's glaciers—the facts

There are more mountain glaciers in Alaska than in the rest of the inhabited world altogether.
Five percent of Alaska is covered by glaciers and ice fields.
The largest glacier, the Malaspina, covers 840 square miles (2,176 sq km).
The Muir glacier is two miles (3.2 km) wide.
Glaciers move because of their weight. They cut deep valleys in the earth. They advance every winter and retreat in the summer.
Between 1991 and 1994 the giant Columbia Glacier retreated more than a mile (1.6 km).

Carmen Melvin is from Miami, Florida. She's on vacation in Alaska and she's taken a "flightseeing" trip to a glacier. The helicopter has landed on the glacier.

Guide: This way…watch where you're going, please. Our insurance company doesn't want you to hurt yourselves!

Carmen: This is incredible!

Guide: Isn't it great? Watch your step, and stay close by me—that is, unless you want to fall into a crevasse. There are crevasses hundreds of feet deep over there. We're going to begin by walking over to look at them.

Carmen: There's so much ice! And they keep telling us about global warming, you know, that the earth is getting hotter.

Guide: Well, I've been doing this job for five years, and the glacier **has** retreated. It used to be half a mile longer.

Carmen: Oh, really?

Guide: Sure. Unless it begins snowing more during the winters, it'll be gone in 50 years.

Carmen: What's the reason for that?

Guide: We can't say. Farther north, some glaciers are still advancing. Maybe it's the local weather here in southeast Alaska, not the world climate. Unless we do more research, we won't know.

Carmen: People say it's the greenhouse gases. You know, if every car carried one more passenger, the United States would use less gasoline.

Guide: Well, maybe. If everyone planted one tree a year things would improve, and if we all walked instead of driving the air would be cleaner…and I guess we'd all be healthier. But you can't measure it, really.

Carmen: So in 50 years' time this will all be gone?

Guide: Right…unless the winters start getting colder.

Carmen: Colder winters? How do you feel about that here in Alaska? Aren't they cold enough for you?

Guide: Sure! But I wouldn't live here unless I liked snow and ice. And tourists wouldn't come here unless there were glaciers. And believe me, we need the tourist business.

Exercise 1

Rewrite these sentences. Change *if … not* to *unless*.
If it doesn't get colder, the glacier will disappear.
Unless it gets colder, the glacier will disappear.
1. If there isn't more snow, the glacier will retreat.
2. He wouldn't live there if he didn't like ice and snow.
3. If there were no glaciers, many tourists wouldn't visit Alaska.
4. If we don't stop using so much energy, the world will get warmer.
5. If we don't stop destroying trees, the world will get warmer.
6. If you don't watch your step, you'll have an accident.
7. If you don't take the helicopter trip, you'll regret it.
8. He wouldn't be a guide if he didn't know a lot about glaciers.

Exercise 2

Discuss: Do you think the world is getting warmer? What can we do about it?

Make sentences with *if … not* or *unless*.

THE READERS' PAGE --------

WHAT WOULD YOU HAVE DONE?

Last week we invited you, the readers, to write and tell us about things that had happened to you, or things that you had heard about. We wanted stories where people just didn't know what to do next! Here are the stories that interested us the most!

THAT'S MY COFFEE...OR WAS

I was at a counter in a restaurant in a small western town. I had just been served a cup of coffee. Suddenly this huge man—he looked like a boxer—came over, picked up my coffee, drank it, banged the cup down on the table, stared at me, and then walked away without saying anything. I suppose I should have said something, but I was scared stiff! I didn't know what to do! What would you have done?

Stanley Wempe
Carbondale, IL

IN DEEP WATER

I was driving through Oregon on my vacation. It was a very hot day, and I stopped at a small, deserted beach. I didn't have my bathing suit with me, but it was early in the morning and there were no people or houses in sight. So I took off my clothes and swam out in the ocean in my underwear. I'm a very strong swimmer. I floated on my back, closed my eyes, and relaxed in the water. When I looked back at the beach, several cars had arrived and there were 20 or 30 people sitting on the sand having a picnic! What would you have done?

Jane Dare
Spokane, WA

THAT'S A NO-NO

I heard a great story about the Reverend Billy Cracker. He'd gone to London to speak at a large meeting. Anyway, when he stepped off the plane there were a lot of reporters and TV cameras. The first

question one of the reporters asked was, "Do you intend to visit any nightclubs in London?" Reverend Cracker smiled at the reporter. "Are there any nightclubs in London?" he answered innocently. The next morning the headline in one of the London papers was "Cracker's first question on arrival in London—Are there any nightclubs?" How would you have felt?

Rev. Aural Richards
Columbia, SC

STRANGERS IN THE NIGHT

My story isn't funny at all. It was a very frightening experience. You see, one night I woke up suddenly. I heard the tinkle of broken glass from downstairs, and I heard the window opening. Then I heard two voices! My wife woke up too. She told me to do something. A couple of days before, there had been a report about a burglary in the local paper. The burglars had been interrupted, and they had beaten up the homeowner. They'd nearly killed him. I was trembling with fear. I just didn't know what to do. In the end, I didn't go down, and they stole the sterling silverware we had inherited from my mother. Was I right? What would you have done?

Lorenzo Machado
Abilene, TX

DEEP-FRIED

I had parked my car at a local shopping mall, and I was taking a shortcut through the side door of a restaurant. Halfway across the restaurant, I spotted my father eating a hamburger and french fries—he often eats there. I sneaked up behind him, put my hand over his shoulder, took a french fry off the plate, dipped it in the ketchup, and ate it. Then I realized that the man was not my father! I was so embarrassed! I couldn't say a word! What would you have done?

Cheryl Redburn
Minneapolis, MN

Look at this:

Would you have said anything?
What would you have done?

I	'd	have	said	something.
	would	done		
	wouldn't			anything.

Exercise 1

Write sentences about each of the five stories.
I'd have (said)....
I wouldn't have (done)....

Exercise 2

Tell the story of an interesting, surprising,
or embarrassing experience you have had or heard about.

says (sah2) I'd have sent
said (sehd) id ov sent

A bad day at the office

Amy: What was wrong this morning?
Tim: Wrong? What do you mean?
Amy: You walked straight past me.
Tim: Really? Where?
Amy: By that newsstand on 1st Street.
Tim: I'm really sorry, Amy. I just didn't see you.
Amy: Come on, Tim. You must have. I was waving!
Tim: No, honestly, I didn't see you. If I had seen you, I would've said hello.

Rob: Tim, have you sent that fax to Japan?
Tim: No, I haven't.
Rob: Why haven't you done it yet? It's urgent.
Tim: Because you didn't ask me to do it.
Rob: I didn't?
Tim: No, you didn't. If you had asked me, I'd have sent it.

Tim: What's the matter, Debbie? You don't look well.
Debbie: No. I've had a terrible cold. It's better today, though.
Tim: Hmm…I had a bad cold last week.
Debbie: I know, and you gave it to everyone in the office. I wouldn't have come to work if I'd had a cold like that.

Rob: Tim, did you type this letter or did Akiko?
Tim: I did. Is there something wrong?
Rob: Take a look. This should be $400,000. You typed $40,000.
Tim: *Oops.* I'm really sorry.
Rob: And the customer's name should be "Snelling," not "Smelling."
Tim: Oh, no! Did I put that?
Rob: If I hadn't noticed it, we could have lost the order!

Dana: Hi, Tim. Did you have a good day today?
Tim: No, not really. I'm glad it's over. Everything went wrong.
Dana: Really?
Tim: Yeah, I made a lot of mistakes in typing, then I forgot to send a fax, and Amy got upset because I ignored her on the street.
Dana: Why was that?
Tim: If I hadn't gone to bed late, it wouldn't have been such an awful day.

Exercise 1

He didn't see her. He didn't say hello.
If he had seen her, he would have said hello.
He would have said hello if he had seen her.

Do the same:
1. He didn't recognize her. He didn't stop.
2. He didn't notice her. He didn't stop.
3. He didn't see her waving. He didn't wave back.

Exercise 2

Have you sent the fax?
If you had asked me, I would have sent it.

Do the same:
1. Have you mailed the letters?
2. Have you photocopied the report?
3. Have you typed the contract?

Exercise 3

He had a bad cold, but he came to work.
I wouldn't have come to work if I had had a cold.

Do the same:
1. She had a headache, but she stayed at work.
2. He had a sore throat, but he worked all day.
3. She had a toothache, but she didn't go to the dentist.

Exercise 4

He noticed the error. They didn't lose the order.
If he hadn't noticed the error, they could have lost the order.

Do the same:
1. He noticed the spelling mistake. They didn't upset the customer.
2. He saw the typo in time. They didn't send the letter.
3. He checked the address. They didn't mail it.

Exercise 5

I went to a party./I went to bed late./ I forgot to set the alarm./I got up late./ I missed the bus./I was late for work./ I've had a bad day./I forgot to send a fax./I made a mistake in typing.

If I hadn't gone to a party, none of these things would have happened.
If I hadn't gone to a party, I wouldn't have gone to bed late.

Write seven sentences.

A Saturday afternoon

Laura felt slightly uneasy as the guard unlocked the gates and waved her through. The Blitzkopf Clinic was, after all, the most exclusive institution of its type in the country. She parked her car outside the main entrance of the sterile white main building. She paused on the steps to look at the beautiful flower gardens. An old man was watering the flower bed beside the steps. He smiled at her.

Old man: Good afternoon. Are you a new patient?
Laura: Oh, I'm not a patient. I'm just here to do some research…I wonder if you could tell me the way to Dr. Blitzkopf's office?
Old man: Certainly. Just go through the main door, turn left, walk down to the end of the hall, and it's the last door on the right.
Laura: Thank you very much.

Dr. Blitzkopf was expecting her. He had been looking forward to meeting his new research assistant. Dr. Blitzkopf showed her around. He was obviously very proud of his clinic, and Laura was impressed by the relaxed and informal atmosphere.

For the next few weeks, Laura spent the mornings interviewing patients and the afternoons in the flower gardens, writing up the results of her research. Some of the patients were withdrawn and depressed; some seemed almost normal. She found it hard to believe that all of them had been considered too dangerous to live in normal society.

Laura often saw the old man in the straw hat. He spent most of his time working in the flower gardens, but he always stopped to speak to her. She found out that his name was Edward Beale. He was a gentle and mild-mannered man, with clear, blue, honest eyes, white hair, and a pinkish complexion. He always looked pleased with life. She became particularly curious about him. One night, at dinner, she asked about Mr. Beale.

Dr. Blitzkopf: Ah, yes, Edward. Nice old guy. He's been here longer than anybody.
Laura: What's wrong with him?
Dr. Blitzkopf: Nothing. His family put him here 40 years ago. They never come to visit him, but the bills are always paid on time.
Laura: But what had he done?
Dr. Blitzkopf: He burned down his school when he was 17. Over the next few years there were a number of mysterious fires in his neighborhood, but the family did nothing until he tried to set fire to the family mansion. He was in here the next day. Edward never protested.

Laura: And that was 40 years ago?!
Dr. Blitzkopf: I'm afraid so.
Laura: But he couldn't still be dangerous!
Dr. Blitzkopf: No. If he'd wanted to start a fire, he could have done it at any time.

Laura was shocked by the story. She wrote letters to Edward's family, but never received a reply. He had never been officially certified as insane, so he could leave at any time. Dr. Blitzkopf let her talk to Edward.

Laura: Edward, have you ever thought about leaving this place?
Edward: No. This is my home. And anyway, I have nowhere else to go.
Laura: But wouldn't you like to go into town sometimes?
Edward: I suppose it would be nice. But I wouldn't want to stay away for long. I've spent 40 years working on this garden. What would happen to it if I weren't here?

Laura realized that it would be unkind to make him leave. But when she found out that the next Saturday was his birthday, she arranged with the staff to give him a party. They wanted it to be a surprise, and Dr. Blitzkopf agreed to let him go out for the afternoon. Edward left at two o'clock. He seemed quite excited. They expected him to return about four o'clock. The cook had made a birthday cake.

Laura was standing in the window when she saw him. He was walking up the drive toward the house, whistling cheerfully. Behind him, above the trees, thick black columns of smoke were beginning to rise slowly into the clear blue sky.

Exercise 1

Find words that mean:
1. the skin's color and appearance
2. socially restricted, snobbish
3. lifeless
4. socially or emotionally detached

Exercise 2

Discuss: Who do you think was responsible for the fire? To what extent were these people responsible: Edward, his family, Dr. Blitzkopf, Laura?

VACATION USA

WESTAIR Airlines

THE GOLDEN WEST • 14 DAYS
San Francisco • 5 nights
Las Vegas • 2 nights
Los Angeles • 6 nights

Can you see yourself riding a cable car in San Francisco, winning a fortune in the casinos of Las Vegas, and walking with the stars on Hollywood Boulevard? WESTAIR invites you to spend two unforgettable weeks in California and Nevada and enjoy the glitter and the glamour of the Golden West.

Marisol is Colombian and married to George Marek, an American teaching in Colombia. They've just returned to Colombia and George is telling his friends at work about their trip.

"We had a great time, but it was pretty tiring. We went on most of the tours because Marisol didn't want to miss anything. I really felt we needed more time. If we went again, we'd stay longer. We would have spent more time in San Francisco and less time in Los Angeles if we'd had a choice. Los Angeles was a little disappointing. We went on a tour of Beverly Hills to see the houses of the stars. But unless you had studied film history, you would never have heard of most of them! Generally speaking, the hotels, food, and service were excellent. Marisol found Americans to be very friendly. We probably took too much luggage. Clothes in California were so cheap! It would have been a good idea to take along an empty suitcase! If I'd done that, the savings on clothes would almost have paid for half of the airfare! Well, not really…."

Imagine

San Francisco with the Golden Gate Bridge, Chinatown, Japantown, cable cars climbing up the steep hills, restaurants serving food from the four corners of the world. Tour Monterey, Carmel, and the wine country of Napa and Sonoma.

Los Angeles, home of the movie industry, Sunset Boulevard, Beverly Hills—and of course—the stars! Choose from any number of tours—the wonderful world of Disneyland, Universal Studios, or a shopping spree on Rodeo Drive.

Las Vegas, the gambling capital of the world! Las Vegas never sleeps and the entertainment is the finest in the world. There's an optional flight over the spectacular Grand Canyon.

This exciting three-city tour offers you a golden opportunity to experience the special atmosphere of the Golden West.

The Rizzos, a retired couple from Bangor, Maine, were on the tour with the Mareks. Florence Rizzo was asked about the trip.

"We'd been looking forward to this trip for years, and it was the vacation of a lifetime. I think we enjoyed Las Vegas the most, but two nights were probably enough! If we'd stayed there much longer, we'd have lost all our money! Disneyland is a "must" for anyone with children. If only we'd had our grandchildren with us! They would have loved it! We went on some of the tours, and we could have gone on more, but you can't see everything, can you? I loved the food in California. You know, all those salads and fresh vegetables! We wouldn't have gone on this trip unless it had been an escorted tour group. We're not as young as we used to be, and we couldn't have done it on our own. Everyone, however, was so helpful to us."

🎧 Listening

Listen to the ad for Dr. Bronner's Hot Springs Spa, and answer these questions.

1. In what city is Dr. Bronner's Hot Springs Spa located?
2. How much does a complete health treatment cost?
3. How much are the rooms at Dr. Bronner's?
4. What do the rooms come with?
5. What street is Dr. Bronner's on?
6. What number should you call for reservations?

Food for thought

"One man's meat is another man's poison."
TRADITIONAL PROVERB

There is a wide range of nutritious foods in the world. However, eating habits differ from country to country. In some societies certain foods are taboo. An eccentric millionaire once invited guests from several countries to a banquet and offered them this menu. All the foods are popular in some parts of the world, but are not eaten in others.

APPETIZERS
Snails
Frogs' legs
Pigs' feet
Oysters
Caviar
100-year-old eggs
Tripe (cow's stomach)
Blood sausage
Live sea urchins

SOUPS
Bird's-nest soup
Shark-fin soup
Seaweed soup

FISH
Octopus
Jellied eels

MAIN COURSES
Cow brains
Whole stuffed camel
Grilled songbirds
Roast snake
Bat stew
Horsemeat
Kangaroo
Whale
Roast Dog
Pork
Beef
Lamb
Veal
Alligator steak

DESSERT
Chocolate-covered ants
Salad of flower petals

If you had been there, which items could you have eaten? Which items would you have eaten? Which items couldn't you have eaten? Why not?

Do you know which countries they are popular in? Would you eat them if you were starving?

What unusual things are eaten in your country? Does your country/region/state have a national/regional dish? How do you make it?

"Part of the secret of success in life is to eat what you like, and let the food fight it out inside you."
MARK TWAIN

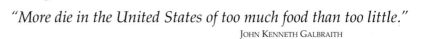

Here are some common ideas about food:
Eating carrots is good for the eyes.
Fish is good for the brain.
Eating cheese at night makes you dream.
Garlic keeps you from getting colds.
Drinking coffee keeps you from sleeping.
Yogurt makes you live long.
An apple a day keeps the doctor away.
Warm milk helps you go to sleep.
A cup of tea settles your stomach.
Brown eggs taste better than white ones.

Have you heard similar expressions?
Do you agree or disagree with them?

"More die in the United States of too much food than too little."
JOHN KENNETH GALBRAITH

At different times in different countries there have been different ideas of beauty. The rich would always want to look fat in a society where food was scarce, and to look thin in a society where food was plentiful. The current interest in losing weight is because of fashion as well as health. However, overeating causes a variety of illnesses.

Do you know what they are? Are you overweight, average, or underweight? Does it bother you? Have you ever been on a diet? What did you eat? What foods should you eat/not eat if you want to lose weight? What should you eat if you want to put on weight?

"One should eat to live, not live to eat."
MOLIERE

"Year by year, while the world's population has increased, the food supply has increased more. (But) … supplies of nourishing food could be enormously increased if, in the richer countries of the world, people were prepared to eat some of the food they feed to their pigs and cattle … and to their pet dogs and cats."
DR. MAGNUS PYKE

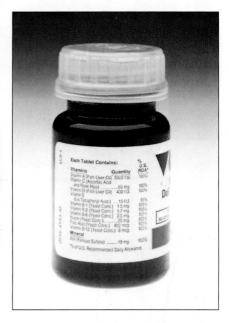

L.B. Waspson: Yes?

Judy: Your call from New York's on line one. Paris has just come through on line two, and there's a call from Tokyo on line four.

L.B.: Ask them to call back tomorrow, Judy. Tell them…tell them I'm not here. It's too late. I wish I wasn't here. I've had enough today.

Judy: But they're urgent, all of them.

L.B.: Do you know something, Judy? I wish I was at home now, in front of the television with a cup of hot chocolate.

Paul: Look at that! It's pouring again, and I have to walk to the bus stop.

Diane: Well at least it's not snow.

Paul: It's all right for Waspson. His limousine is downstairs waiting to take him home.

Diane: Yeah. I wish I had a chauffeur-driven limousine.

Paul: I wish I had a car, any car. I'm going to get soaked tonight!

Tony: Hi, Jane. Still here?

Jane: Yes. I'm waiting to see Waspson.

Tony: You don't usually work late.

Jane: I wish I wasn't working this evening. There's a good game on TV.

Tony: Oh, well. Maybe he'll call you in soon.

Jane: I hope he does!

Alan: Haven't you left yet?

Lorraine: No. I wish I had. I can't go until I've finished this report.

Alan: Can't you do it tomorrow?

Lorraine: I wish I could, but Waspson wants it tonight.

Shirley: How are you doing, Joe?

Joe: Oh, hi, Shirley. I don't feel like working tonight.

Shirley: Neither do I. I hate this kind of work.

Joe: Why do you do it then?

Shirley: I wish I didn't have to! But we need the money. My husband's out of work again.

Joe: I know what you mean. I wish I'd learned how to type, or something like that.

Shirley: We can all wish! I dropped out of school at 16. I wish I hadn't, but I never got good grades and I hated it. Kids have it really easy in school nowadays. I wish we'd had more of a chance. I'd never have ended up cleaning offices…

Joe: Come on, Shirley, let's try to finish early and get out of here.

Police Officer: Look at that, Sergeant. There are still lights on in the insurance company again.

Sergeant: Yes, it looks nice and warm, doesn't it? I sometimes wish I worked there.

Officer: You do? Really?

Sergeant: Uh-huh. Sometimes. A nice office, a desk, lots of people around…. It can't be bad.

Officer: And the boss's limo outside.

Sergeant: Still, you know what they say: "The grass is always greener on the other side."

Officer: I suppose you're right, Sarge. Hey, that limousine is in front of a fire hydrant.

Sergeant: Oh, yeah. Give him a parking ticket, Lucy. He can afford it!

Exercise 1

1. I wish I was on vacation.
I wish I was in Hawaii.
Where do you wish you were now?
Do you wish you were in bed?/at home?/on the beach?
2. I'm a student.
I wish I was an actor.
What do you wish you were?

Exercise 2

I don't have a car.
I wish I had a car.

Make five sentences.

Exercise 3

It's raining.
I wish it wasn't raining.
She's working.
She wishes she wasn't working.

Continue.
1. The phones are ringing.
2. It's snowing.
3. She's sitting in an office.
4. He's waiting.

Exercise 4

She hasn't finished yet.
She wishes she had finished.
I didn't learn how to type.
I wish I had learned how to type.

Continue.
1. They haven't done their homework.
2. She dropped out of school at 16.
3. I haven't seen that movie.
4. He lost his wallet.

The happiest days of your life?

Some people say that your days in school are the happiest days of your life. Here are five people talking about their experiences.

Wade Hamlin is a successful self-employed builder.

"School? It's a waste of time mostly—at least it was for me. I quit after my sophomore year in college because I stopped hoping that I would ever learn anything. I wanted to start earning a living—in the real world. The biggest problem with school is the teachers. If I had listened to my teachers, I would know all about Shakespeare and what day the Civil War started and how to conjugate Spanish verbs and how to prove the Pythagorean theorem and all that junk. But I wouldn't know anything about how to make a business deal or raise my kids or anything that's really important. I'm sorry I went to school at all."

Anne Marie Johnson is the personnel manager of a department store.

"I loved school. I was a straight-A student almost every year, but I didn't spend all my time studying. I participated in a lot of extracurricular activities and sports too. I was in student government both in high school and in college. I was always sorry when summer vacation started—three months with no school! Most kids liked vacations more than school, but not me. Some of my friends in high school didn't go to college, but they regret it now. Some of them would have done well if they had been encouraged to go. I only regret not going to graduate school after I got my bachelor's degree. I've started an MBA at night, but it's not the same. Work is all right, but I miss the friends and the fun that went along with the studying."

Craig Phillips is a Wall Street stockbroker.

"I went to prep school, and then I went to Harvard. I guess you could say I had the best education money could buy, but it wasn't easy. We had to study very hard, and a lot was expected of us. The thing I remember most is the friendship. The friends I made then are still my friends today. Most of us were together in prep school and then at Harvard too. Sports were very important for me. I believe that team sports teach people to work together, and competition with another team brings out the best in people…. Anyway, discipline was stricter then. It's too bad that has changed. Maybe young people would be better behaved nowadays if there was more discipline in the schools. My biggest regret is that I didn't have the family life other boys had. After age 12, I only saw my family at Christmas and in the summer.

Colleen McGrath is a factory worker.

"School was just another part of neighborhood life. My brothers and sisters and I went to a parochial elementary school three blocks from home. Later we had to take a bus to the public high school, but it was only a ten-minute ride. And then we all went to the local community college. I wish my kids could do that. I have to take the youngest in the car to the big elementary school across the river. A school bus picks up the other two who are in junior high school, and it takes them almost an hour each way. I wish things hadn't changed so much."

🎧 Listening

Listen to Kaye Wilson talk about her school days, and answer these questions.
Where did she go to high school?
Where did she live?
What courses does she wish she had taken?
Why did her parents send her to a fancy girls' college?
What does she do now?
What would she be if she had taken the courses she had wanted?

Exercise

What about your days in school? What do/did you like?
What don't/didn't you like?
What about sports?/discipline?/subjects you liked and didn't like?/teachers?/extracurricular activities?

New Year's Eve

Western New Year's Day January 1

Chinese New Year Sometime between mid-January and mid-February

Jewish New Year Rosh Hashanah – sometime in September or October

Islamic New Year 1 Muharram – sometime in May, June, or July

Ask and answer these questions:

Do you celebrate New Year?
Ask "When?" Ask "Where?" Ask "How?"
What do people do on New Year's Eve?
Are there any special foods or drinks for New Year's Eve or New Year's Day?
Do people give each other presents?
Do people make wishes?
Do people make New Year's resolutions
(promises to do something or change something about themselves)?

Naomi: It's ten minutes before midnight, and we're going over live to Times Square in New York City. There are a quarter of a million people out there, and they're all waiting to celebrate the New Year. Adam Vasquez is going to talk to just a few of them. How are you doing, Adam?

Adam: Great, Naomi, just great. As you can see, there's a real party atmosphere down here! I'm going to move through the crowd and talk to some of the people who have come here. Excuse me. Can I speak to you for a moment, please?

Robin: Sure.

Adam: What are your names, and where are you from?

Robin: I'm Robin, and this is my boyfriend, Phil. We're from New Jersey.

Adam: New Jersey? Just across the river. Are you having a good time?

Robin: Great time. No problems. We've watched the ball drop on TV ever since we were kids. This is the first time we've actually come in person. It's great. Really great.

Adam: Do you work in New Jersey?

Robin: Yeah. I'm a nurse.

Adam: OK, Robin. I want to ask you one question. Just one! If you could have one wish for next year, what would you wish for?

Robin: A serious wish or just kidding around?

Adam: You choose.

Robin: OK. If I could have one wish, I'd wish for three more wishes!

Adam: That's against the rules, Robin.

Robin: Well, seriously, I'd wish for an end to famine and starvation everywhere.

Adam: Great. Thanks, and a happy new year to both of you.

🎧 Listening

Adam interviewed four more people.
Listen and complete the chart.

INTERVIEW	NAME	OCCUPATION	WISH
1			
2			
3			
4			

Exercise 1

Answer the following questions:

If you could travel anywhere in the world, where would you go? Why?

If you could live anywhere in the world, where would you live? Why?

If you could meet any famous person, who would you meet?

If you could have any job, what would it be?

If you could have any kind of car, what kind would it be?

Exercise 2

Discuss: If you could have one wish, what would you wish for?

T: Now, 006. I want you to look at these pictures carefully. At last we have the chance to break the biggest crime syndicate in the world—SMASH. Look at the man on the right. He's the one we've been after for years.

006: Who is he?

T: We think he's the one that controls SMASH. He's certainly the one that ordered the murder of 003, the one that planned the hijacking of the airplane full of world leaders, and the one that organized the biggest drug-smuggling operation in the world.

006: Do we know his name?

T: Otto Krugerand.

006: Otto Krugerand. And who's that standing behind him?

T: Ah, Slojob. He's the bodyguard who travels everywhere with Krugerand, and the only person he trusts. He's an expert assassin. He's the one who fed 004 to the alligators.

006: How charming! What about the woman?

T: Don't you recognize her?

006: Mala Powers! She's the one who arranged the pipeline explosion and then vanished into thin air!

T: She's also Krugerand's wife and the only pilot he allows to fly his private plane.

006: Who's the little guy wearing thick glasses?

T: That's Professor Peratoff, the mad scientist who defected from Moldania. He's an expert on laser technology and the first man who's been able to perfect a space laser weapon.

Krugerand is planning to build a private space rocket which could put a satellite into orbit. Do you understand the importance of this, 006? If they got a laser weapon into space, they could blackmail the world!

T: Take a look at this picture, 006.

006: It's an oil rig.

T: It looks like it, doesn't it? It belongs to Krugerand's oil company. It's supposed to be drilling for oil in the Indian Ocean. Below it, there's a vast underwater complex.

006: The superstructure looks odd.

T: In fact, it conceals the launching pad they're going to use for the rocket.

006: That must be a radar scanner, there.

T: Yes. It's the scanner they'll use to track the rocket, but they can also see anything that tries to get near the rig. It's going to be very difficult to get you in, 006.

006: What's the plan, then?

T: We're flying you to California tonight for two weeks of intensive mini-submarine training.

006: That sounds like fun!

Exercise 1

Exercise 2

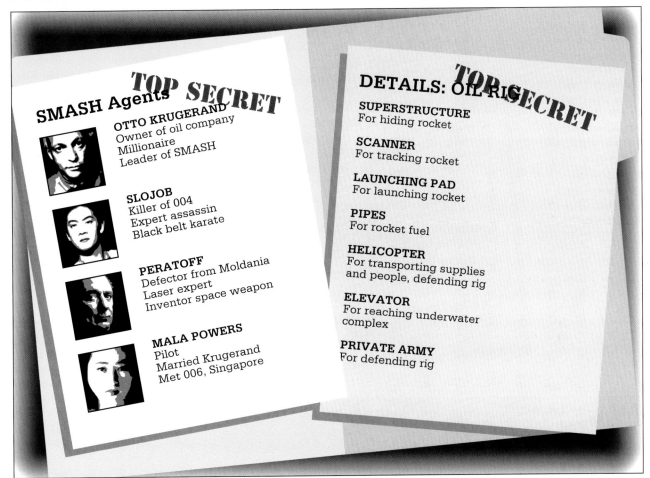

Krugerand's the one | who / that | owns an oil company.

He's the one | who / that | 's a millionaire.

Make more sentences like this about other members of SMASH.

What's that?
It's the scanner | which / that | they'll use to track the rocket.

Make more sentences.

Exercise 3

She's the woman. He met her in Singapore.
She's the woman he met in Singapore.

Continue.
1. 003 was the agent. Slojob killed him.
2. Otto Krugerand's the leader. We've been trying to catch him.
3. That's the laser scanner. They'll use it to track the rocket.
4. Mala Powers is the woman. Otto Krugerand married her.
5. Peratoff is the scientist. SMASH recruited him.
6. They're the people. 006 must stop them.

Exercise 1

Look at the itinerary.
He went to San Diego, where he learned to handle a mini-sub. He went back to Washington, where he was given a transmitter. He was given a transmitter, which was put into the heel of his shoe.

Make complete sentences, using *where* and *which* about 006's itinerary.

ITINERARY FOR 006   TOP SECRET

1. SAN DIEGO
Submarine training center. Learn to handle mini-sub. Board helicopter to go to offshore oil rig.

2. OIL RIG
Study design of the rig.
Practice controlling the submarine.

3. WASHINGTON
Get latest information, false papers and identity. Get transmitter. Transmitter put into heel of shoe. Suicide pill in tooth.

4. LONDON
Report to M on operation. Obtain cigarette lighter–it can be used as a flame thrower.

5. MOMBASSA, KENYA
Board a freighter–freighter carries coffee.

6. A POINT EAST OF THE SEYCHELLES
Rendezvous with aircraft carrier carrying a mini-sub. Transfer mini-sub to freighter.

7. A POINT 50 MILES FROM OTTO'S RIG
Submarine put in water. 006 boards it.

When 006 reached the rig, he climbed up one of the towers. He needed to change out of his wet suit. He went into an empty cabin, found some clothes just his size, and put them on. Suddenly, the guard whose cabin he was searching came in. Everything went dark.

006 woke up with his hands tied behind his back. His head was throbbing. He was apparently in some kind of control room. In the room were Otto Krugerand, Slojob, Mala, and the guard whose clothes he was wearing. A beautiful woman, whose hands were also tied, was lying beside him. She was Pic Welles, an American agent 006 had met in Washington. 006 glanced at his watch. The explosive device he'd put on the rig was timed to explode in 40 minutes.

"Welcome, Commander Fleming. We've been expecting you," Otto said, smiling. "Unfortunately we won't have time to show you around.

Slojob will take you to feed the sharks. They must be very hungry by now."

Slojob escorted them to Krugerand's private apartment. One wall was made of thick glass. Behind it, 006 could see the dark shapes of the sharks swimming around. Slojob pushed the two agents up a spiral staircase to a platform above the shark tank. He was careful to keep his gun trained on them all the time.

"You wouldn't refuse us a last cigarette, would you, Slojob?" 006 asked.

"I don't smoke," Slojob grinned. "And you shouldn't, either. It's bad for your health."

"Now, come on, Slojob. There are some cigarettes and a lighter in my jacket pocket."

"OK. But don't try anything." Slojob reached into 006's pocket and took out the cigarettes and lighter. He took one cigarette out of the pack, pushed it into 006's mouth, and put the pack back into 006's pocket. Slojob pressed the lighter with his thumb. The sudden force of the flame took him by surprise. At that moment, 006 kicked him, and his gun fell to the floor. Slojob tumbled backward and disappeared forever into the tank of sharks.

The lighter had dropped to the floor and was still burning. 006 was able to burn through the ropes that held his hands. He quickly untied Pic, who picked up Slojob's gun.

"We don't have much time," he said. "Can you fly a helicopter?"

"With my eyes closed," she replied.

"Good. Let's go."

006 and Pic tiptoed into the control room, where Otto and Mala still were. Peratoff had joined them. 006 fired the lighter at the control panel, which exploded and burst into flames. Otto tackled 006, and the lighter flew out of his hand. Mala and Peratoff desperately tried to put out the flames. Pic pointed the gun at Mala, Otto, and Peratoff, and ordered them to lie on the floor. Then she and 006 ran out of the room, locking it behind them. They ran up to the helicopter pad and quickly climbed into the helicopter. The helicopter soared into the sky. A few seconds later there was a massive explosion as the rig blew up.

Host: Our next contestant is Vickie MacLean, who is a student at Portstown High School. OK, Vickie. You have two minutes in which to answer as many questions as possible. If you do not know the answer, say, "Pass." I will then go on to the next question. If you answer incorrectly, I will then give the correct answer. You will get one point for each correct answer. Are you ready?

Vickie: Yes.

Host: Can you name the president of the United States whose early career began as a radio sports announcer?

Vickie: Uh—Reagan. Ronald Reagan.

Host: Correct. What is an instrument that shows the direction of north?

Vickie: A compass?

Host: Exactly. What is the date when France celebrates their revolution of 1789?

Vickie: The fourteenth of July.

Host: Correct. What do we call a person who always expects the best to happen?

Vickie: Uh—an optimist.

Host: Correct. Can you tell me the language that was spoken in the Roman Empire?

Vickie: Italian?

Host: No, wrong. The correct answer is Latin. What kind of person do people visit when they want advice about their marriage?

Vickie: Pass.

Host: Who was the Egyptian queen whose beauty was famous throughout the world?

Vickie: Cleopatra.

Host: That's correct. What's the kind of school where very rich people send their children before college?

Vickie: Uh—private school?

Host: Can you be more exact?

Vickie: No. I can't think of it.

Host: I'm afraid I can't give you that. We were looking for "prep" school or "preparatory" school. Now can you tell me… (*Ding*) I've started, so I'll finish. Can you tell me the name of the French emperor whose final battle was at Waterloo?

Vickie: Napoleon Bonaparte.

Host: Correct. And at the end of that round Vickie MacLean has scored six points. You passed on one—the kind of person people visit when they want advice about their marriage is a marriage counselor. Thank you. Can we have our next contestant, please?

Exercise 1

Now practice the game with a partner.

QUESTIONS

1. What's a person who breaks into a house and steals things?
2. Who was the boxer whose most famous words were "I am the greatest"?
3. What's a place where people go to watch sports or see concerts?
4. What is the day when Christians celebrate the birth of Jesus?
5. What's the place where you go to wait for the announcement for a flight?
6. What's a tool that is used for digging?
7. Can you tell me the unusual system of public transportation that is used in San Francisco?
8. Can you name the American president who was assassinated in 1963?
9. Name the two young lovers whose tragic story was made into a play by Shakespeare.
10. What do we call a piece of art or furniture that is over 100 years old?

burglar/Muhammad Ali/a stadium/
Christmas Day/a gate/a shovel/
cable car/John F. Kennedy/Romeo
and Juliet/an antique

Exercise 2

Work with a partner. One of you uses List A, the other uses List B. Each of you writes down ten questions using the words *who/which/where/when/whose* given in parentheses in the list. Your questions must ask for the answer provided in the list. For example:

Neil Armstrong (who)
Q: Can you tell me the name of the first man who walked on the moon?
A: Neil Armstrong.

widower (whose)
Q: What do you call a man whose wife has died?
A: A widower.

Then, with books closed, ask your partner the questions you have prepared. Your partner will then ask you to answer the questions he or she has prepared.

LIST A	LIST B
Neil Armstrong (who)	widower (whose)
sailor (who)	Columbus (who)
receipt (which)	a cover letter (which)
submarine (which)	driver's license (which)
newsstand (where)	a shopping mall (where)
casino (where)	silver wedding anniversary (when)
golden wedding anniversary (when)	Marilyn Monroe (who)
Valentine's Day (when)	Romeo (whose)
Josephine Bonaparte (whose)	a wallet (where)

The Middleburg Herald

Vol. LXVI No. 262   Thursday, September 25, 1997   Price 30¢

DANIEL STRIKES CAROLINA COAST

CAPE HATTERAS, NC, Sept 25 (WP). Hurricane Daniel, which is this season's fourth hurricane, became the first to hit this coastal area in five years. Gale winds, which at times reached a force of 100 m.p.h., downed power lines and destroyed beach houses. Flooding, which was caused by torrential rains and high waves, left highways and roads impassable through last night. Coastal residents, who had been evacuated to inland locations, waited for the floodwaters to subside before they returned to their homes, which might have been damaged by the storm.

Governor Fran Scott called out the National Guard to help the Red Cross, which is working around the clock in the emergency. The guard will also assist local efforts to reopen the area's streets and roads, which were blocked by fallen trees and other debris.

The governor, who toured the hardest hit areas by helicopter, asked the Federal Government to declare the area a national disaster. The president, who is spending the weekend at Camp David, is expected to make a declaration today. The declaration, which will apply only to the hardest-hit areas on the coast, will make millions of Federal dollars available for emergency relief. The governor has already announced emergency small-business loans, which will help supermarkets and other businesses make needed repairs.

More photos and related articles on page A6

Sheridan Street Holdout Stands Firm
Mayor Unable to Persuade Woman and Dogs to Move

MIDTONVILLE, Sept. 24 (PAI). Mrs. Florence Hamilton, who has gained national attention in her fight to remain in her home, is still refusing to move, and the "Battle of Sheridan Street" continues. Midtonville Mayor Ethan Cox, who had not taken part in the battle until today, joined Housing Authority Director Hilda Martinez in front of Mrs. Hamilton's house at 2:30 this afternoon.

The house, which the Housing Authority wants to demolish to make way for a large public housing development, now stands alone. The Mayor, who was elected on his promises to put people, especially the poor, above other concerns, spoke to Mrs. Hamilton by bullhorn, asking her to come and meet with him. He was forced to retreat to his limousine, which stood at the curb, doors open, when Mrs. Hamilton answered by turning loose two of her dogs.

Mrs. Hamilton, whose plight has inspired a wave of public support, repeated her refusals to move in an interview with reporters later.
(continued on page A9)

Mystery Explosion In Indian Ocean
Oil Rig Destroyed in Blast

SEYCHELLES ISLANDS, SEPT. 25 (PAI). An oil rig in the Indian Ocean exploded mysteriously yesterday. The oil rig, which had been drilling a test well, belonged to the Krugerand Corporation. A series of bright flashes, which were observed by ships 60 miles away, preceded shock waves of unusual force. Several ships, which rushed to the rescue, have been searching for survivors, but so far none have been found. It is not known how many people were working on the rig at the time of the explosion. Krugerand Corp. which is based in Switzerland, would not comment on the explosion. *(continued on page A8)*

🎧 **Listening 1**

Listen to the news item and answer these questions.
1. What happened to Caroline Newton last Monday?
2. What do her parents do for a living?
3. Where was she found?
4. Who called the police?
5. What did the suspects want?

🎧 **Listening 2**

Listen to the news item and answer these questions.
1. Who banned Kural?
2. How have doctors been recommending Kural?
3. Who demanded the tests?
4. What does the drug speed up?

August 15, 1995

Mr. Les Gardner
1339 Elm Avenue
Memphis, TN 38104

Dear Mr. Gardner:

Thank you for your letter of August 1, in which you ask about missing and damaged items in your laundry while staying at our hotel.

We are sorry that you did not find our laundry service satisfactory. May we remind you that the form on which you listed your laundry items states very clearly that the hotel is not responsible for loss or damage, and the plastic bag in which you placed your clothes has the same warning printed in large letters on it.

However, we of course do our best to insure that our guests get all their clothes back from the laundry in good condition. We will review our laundry and dry-cleaning systems to see if we can add further safeguards against loss or damage.

We apologize for any inconvenience you may have experienced and have enclosed a "One Night's Free Stay" voucher, good for you and a guest through December 31, 1997. We hope that you will be staying with us again the next time you are in the area and look forward to serving you.

Sincerely yours,

Greg Larkin
Manager
encl.

To: Makoto Yasuda, Tokyo Office
From: Sharon Underhill, New York Office
Date: January 5, 1998
Subject: Annual International Sales Conference

We are very pleased that you will be able to attend our Annual International Sales Conference from April 20-23, 1998. Almost all our representatives world-wide are planning to attend, most of whom you have already met.

Katherine Horton, with whom you spoke last November, is in charge of all conference logistics. Her fax number is 212-555-2184 and her phone number is 212-555-1400, ext. 221.

Katherine has prepared an attachment to this fax on which she has provided information about the weather in New York in April and recommendations for clothing. She will soon be sending you some information about activities in which you may wish to participate if you plan to be in New York the weekend before the conference.

We have reserved a block of rooms at the Fifth Avenue Hotel, about which we have had very good reports from other visitors. Please fax the attached accommodations request form directly to the hotel by January 31, 1998. If you need to call the hotel, please ask for John Navarro, the manager through whom we have made our arrangements.

Please book your own flights. Once you know the details, please fax the information to Katherine so she can arrange to have you met at the airport.

If you have any questions about travel or accomodations, please call Katherine directly. I am looking forward to seeing you in April.

Exercise 1

He's the man. I wrote to him.
He is the man to whom I wrote. (Formal written)
He's the man who/that I wrote to. (Spoken/informal)

You gave us a form. You listed your laundry items on it.
You gave us a form on which you listed your laundry items. (Formal written)
You gave us a form that you listed your laundry items on. (Spoken/informal)

Transform these sentences into:
  a) formal written style
  b) spoken/informal written style.
1. This is the hotel. We stayed in it.
2. That is the mistake. I am complaining about it.
3. She is the travel agent. We made our arrangements through her.
4. This is the fax. We wrote our agenda on it.
5. These people are the sales staff. You met all of them.
6. That's the hotel. We heard great things about it.
7. Katherine is the manager. Everyone expects so much from her.

Exercise 2

You are Les Gardner. Write his letter of August 1 to Greg Larkin, the manager of the Lighthouse Hotel.

You are Makoto Yasuda. Write a fax to Katherine Horton, giving the details of your flight.

Marjorie and Felix Hernandez have just come back from a vacation in San Francisco. They are showing photographs of their trip to their friends and neighbors, the Winters.

Marjorie: These are our friends. They picked us up at the airport.

Felix: And that's the cable car. It runs on California Street.

Exercise 1

They're the friends. They picked us up at the airport.
They're the friends who picked us up at the airport.

That's the cable car. It runs on California Street.
That's the cable car that runs on California Street.

Continue.
1. This is the park. It was near our hotel.
2. She's the young girl. She sat next to us on the plane.
3. They're our cousins. They live in Mill Valley.
4. That's the museum. It has a mural by Diego Rivera.

Felix: This is Marjorie's friend. We visited her.

Marjorie: This is the car. We rented it for two weeks.

Exercise 2

She's the friend. We visited her.
She's the friend we visited.
She's the friend who we visited.
She's the friend that we visited.

This is the car. We rented it for two weeks.
This is the car we rented for two weeks.
This is the car that we rented for two weeks.

Continue.
1. They're the people. We met them on the tour.
2. This is the picture of the city. We took it from Telegraph Hill.
3. These are the souvenirs. We brought them home.
4. He's the old classmate. We saw him in Chinatown.

Felix: The tour guide was very knowledgeable. She spoke five languages.... And this is BART. BART connects San Francisco to Oakland. It's Oakland's subway.

Exercise 3

The tour guide was very knowledgeable. She spoke five languages.
The tour guide, who spoke five languages, was very knowledgeable.

BART connects San Francisco to Oakland. It's Oakland's subway.
BART, which is Oakland's subway, connects San Francisco to Oakland.

Continue.
1. That hotel is near Union Square. It's the most expensive one in the city.
2. The Golden Gate Bridge has the world's highest bridge towers. It links San Francisco and Marin County.
3. These people were on our tour. They're from New Jersey.
4. The Chocolate Factory makes delicious candy. It's near Fisherman's Wharf.

Felix: You remember my Aunt Molly, don't you, Joe? You haven't seen her since you were about ten. Well, she's 86 this year. We visited her at her apartment in San Francisco. And this is our tour group. The tour was fun. The hotel booked it for us.

Exercise 4

My Aunt Molly was 86 this year. You haven't seen her since you were about ten.
My Aunt Molly, who you haven't seen since you were about ten, was 86 this year.

The tour was fun. The hotel booked it for us.
The tour, which the hotel booked for us, was fun.

Continue.
1. Phil and Eva send their regards. You met them last year.
2. The gifts were expensive. We mailed them home.
3. Cousin Frank took us out for dinner our first night there. I just sent him a thank-you note.
4. The hotel was in a great location. Aunt Molly recommended it.

Marjorie: We bought a beautiful bowl from a potter. His store was in the Japan Center. And we met a lot of nice people. We met two sisters from Detroit. Their parents live in San Francisco.

Exercise 5

We bought a beautiful bowl from a potter. His store was in the Japan Center.
We bought a beautiful bowl from a potter whose store was in the Japan Center.

We met two sisters from Detroit. Their parents live in San Francisco.
We met two sisters from Detroit whose parents live in San Francisco.

Continue.
1. On Monday, I had lunch with a friend. Her boyfriend is a journalist.
2. I bought a book about a young woman. Her father ran for president of the United States.
3. We saw a ballet about a prince. His uncle hated him.
4. On the plane, we saw a movie about two young lovers. Their romance ended happily.

Felix: And this was taken at the restaurant in the hotel. Kevin Costley was sitting at a table next to ours. We saw his movie last week.

Exercise 6

Kevin Costley was sitting at a table next to ours. We saw his movie last week.
Kevin Costley, whose movie we saw last week, was sitting at a table next to ours.

Continue.
1. The Grateful Dead were playing in Golden Gate Park. Their records were famous in the sixties.
2. A woman from our town was at the hotel. Her brother works with me.
3. The tour guide was really excellent. Her name was Eva Sanchez.
4. We visited Phil and Eva. Their apartment is in an old part of the city.

Describing things

STOLEN CAR

A: Police Department. Sergeant Wong speaking.

B: My car's been stolen! It's gone!

A: OK, now, calm down. Let me have your name and address.

B: Richard Lockwood, 4512 Eisenhower Boulevard, Apartment 18J.

A: All right. Now, give me a description of the missing vehicle.

B: Well, it's a '95 Ford Escort—a light-gray, four-door model. Oh, it has a thin dark-blue stripe along the sides and a dent in the left front fender.

A: What's the license plate number?

B: RJG 1224.

A: Hold on just a minute.... Hello? I have some good news and some bad news. The good news is that your car wasn't stolen. It was towed for illegal parking. The bad news is that it will cost you $150 to get it back.

Exercise 1

Describe somebody's car. Describe a car you would like to own.

LOST AND FOUND

A: Union Station Lost and Found Department. Can I help you?

B: Oh, hello. Yes, I hope so. I left my briefcase on the train this morning. I wonder if it has been turned in.

A: Which train?

B: Oh, the 8:40 from Concord.

A: And what does your briefcase look like?

B: Well, it's... uh... an average-sized, rectangular, brown leather attaché case with brass locks.

A: We have quite a few that fit that description. Did it have your name on it?

B: No, not my name, but it has my initials by the handle: J.F.A.

A: Hold on just a minute. Let me take a look.

Exercise 2

Imagine you have lost something. Describe it to a partner without telling him/her what it is. Your partner has to guess.

THE REAL ESTATE AGENT

A: Hello. Donna Woo speaking.

B: Hi, Donna. This is Joyce Fein at Ivy Realty. I think I've found a house you'll be interested in.

A: Oh, terrific! What's it like? Tell me about it.

B: Well, it's in Arrowhead, the section you wanted. It's a split-level, three-bedroom, red-brick house with white trim. It's only six years old and has a large country-style kitchen.

A: How big a yard does it have?

B: It's a one-acre lot with some nice-sized trees and a very pretty flower garden in back. When do you want to see it?

A: Could we meet there tomorrow afternoon? It sounds perfect.

B: Sure thing. Let's make it at two o'clock. Here's the address...

Exercise 3

Describe somebody's house. Describe a house you would like to live in.

Exercise 4

Describe these living rooms.

Describe your ideal living room/kitchen/bedroom/bathroom. Describe the furniture you would put in it and where you would put it.

Describe a restaurant that you've been to.

Describe your classroom.

Note: This chart shows the usual order of adjectives. You won't often find them all in one sentence.

HOW MUCH/ MANY?	WHAT'S IT LIKE?	HOW BIG IS IT?	WHAT SHAPE IS IT?	HOW OLD IS IT?	WHAT COLOR IS IT?		WHAT'S THE PATTERN ON IT?	WHERE'S IT FROM?	WHAT'S IT MADE OF?	WHAT IS IT?
a/an	beautiful	little	square	old	pale	red	checked	French	plastic	scarf
one	nice	small	round	new	light	yellow	striped	English	cotton	shirt
three	ugly	medium-sized	oval	modern	bright	green	plain	Japanese	wood(en)	chair
some	clean	average-sized	rectangular	antique	dark	blue	flowered	Mexican	leather	car
a few	dirty	large	pointed	19th-century		pink	polka-dotted	Italian	gold	house
several	cheap	big	triangular	1930s		black		American	metal	box
a lot of	expensive	long	flat	1995		white		Chinese	paper	

🎧 Listening

Listen to these people talking about their friends. Look at the
example. Complete the other columns.

Name	Donna	Tony	Janet	Bob
Age	late teens			
Build	good figure			
Height	pretty tall			
Hair Color	black			
Hairstyle	long, wavy			
Face	oval-shaped, turned-up nose, full lips			
Eyes	blue, long eyelashes			
Complexion	olive-skinned			
Distinguishing features	dimples			
Dress	jeans/casual			
Personality	talkative, funny			

Look at this:

AGE	BUILD	HEIGHT	HAIR COLOR	HAIRSTYLE	FACE	DISTINGUISHING FEATURES	PERSONALITY
young	heavy	5'7" (5 foot 7)	black	long	thin	beard (M)	nice
middle-aged	thin	medium height	brown	short	long	mustache (M)	quiet
elderly	slim	average height	red	straight	round	sideburns (M)	loud
old	plump	tall	blond	wavy	oval	unshaven/with	reserved
in his/her 30s	medium build	short	ash blond	curly	square	stubble (M)	calm
in his/her late teens	well-built		gray	parted on the left	high cheekbones	clean-shaven (M)	moody
in his/her mid-20s	broad-shouldered		white	neat	high forehead	a scar	(un)sociable
in his/her early 40s	overweight		dyed	windblown	thin lips	a beauty mark	sophisticated
	big-boned		a blond	with braids	full lips	a mole	funny
	petite		a redhead	with bangs	long nose	freckles	cheerful
	skinny		redheaded	swept back	straight nose	dimples	polite
			dark	in a bun (F)	turned-up nose	wrinkles	reliable
			light	ponytail	broken nose	lines	talkative
				bald (M)	Roman nose	glasses	confident
				balding (M)	flat nose	hardly any makeup (F)	aggressive
				thinning	a cleft chin	heavily made-up (F)	friendly
				receding (M)	a pointed chin		shy
					a double chin		

EYES	COMPLEXION	DRESS
blue	pale	scruffy
gray	light	well-dressed
brown	suntanned	casual
long eyelashes	olive (-skinned)	conservative
thick eyebrows/lashes	dark (-skinned)	elegant
bushy eyebrows	black	fashionable
thin eyebrows/lashes		

Exercise

Describe these people. Describe yourself, another student,
and a famous person.

We interrupt our regular television schedule in order to bring you the following presidential debate.

Good evening. I'm Carol Moore. As you know, three people are running for president of the United States. I will introduce them in a moment. In order to be fair, we will allow all three candidates to answer each question. Each candidate will be allowed a one-minute response to make sure everyone gets to express his or her opinion.

And now it gives me great pleasure to introduce our three candidates: Mrs. Victoria Cranston, Mr. Ron Parrow, and Mr. Bob Knoll.

The first area I'd like to ask about is the economy. What are you going to do to make sure the economy improves? Mr. Parrow, we'll start with you.

Parrow: You know, I'm a successful businessman, and I know how to make a lot of money. To get this economy back on its feet, we need to repeal the income tax increases of the last few years. In order to make up for the loss of revenue, I'll put a tax on gasoline. The gas tax would be just ten cents per gallon per year for the next four years. And I'd do a bunch of things to help small business owners. We need to help small businesses in order to increase the number of good jobs. For the purpose of getting the economy moving again, I'll give tax credits to manufacturers. We have to sell things, folks, if we're going to make money. Oh! Am I out of time already?

A few minutes before the presidential debate.

Julie: Come on, Gary. Hurry up. The debate is about to start. How come you're so late?

Gary: The battery was dead. I had to call Al from the garage to give me a jump-start. Then I went back to the garage to get some gas—and to get the battery recharged.

Julie: Oh, no! Do we need a new battery?

Gary: Probably.

Julie: Not another expense! If it's not one thing, it's another! Oh, the debate's starting. We'll talk later.

Exercise 1

garage
He went to the garage to get some gas.

Make sentences with:
1. bank
2. drugstore
3. library
4. newsstand
5. bakery
6. fruit and vegetable store
7. post office
8. supermarket
9. butcher's
10. florist's

Exercise 2

In order to increase the number of good jobs, we need to help small businesses.
For the purpose of increasing the number of good jobs, we need to help small businesses.
We need to help small businesses in order to increase the number of good jobs.
We need to help small businesses for the purpose of increasing the number of good jobs.

Make sentences in each of these four ways about each of Mrs. Cranston's proposals.

Exercise 3

Discuss: What has your government promised to do during its administration?

Mrs. Cranston's Presidential Debate Platform

PROPOSAL	PURPOSE
• Decrease domestic spending	• Reduce deficit
• Simplify tax code	• Treat all taxpayers more fairly
• Develop permanent space station	• Encourage scientific research
• Increase environmental-protection budget	• Develop new techniques to reduce pollution
• Establish a bipartisan commission on education	• Improve schools
• Enforce tougher punishments for criminals	• Encourage a decline in the crime rate
• Reduce nuclear arms	• Promote international peace
• Provide tuition tax credits	• Expand opportunities for low-income families
• Create more child-care centers	• Aid working parents

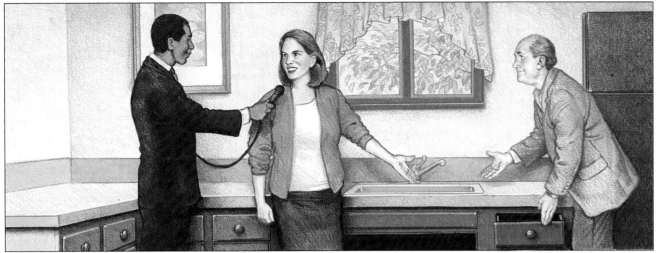

Do-It-Yourself magazine sponsors a contest every summer to find the winner of the annual "Do-It-Yourself" Award. This year a married couple, Rudy and Irene Cipriani, won. A writer from *Do-It-Yourself* is interviewing them at their house.

Writer: Well, I'm very impressed by all the work you've done on your house. How long have you been working on it?

Rudy: We became interested in do-it-yourself several years ago. Our son Paul was in an accident and lost the use of his legs. He's in a wheelchair. We had to make changes so that he could move around the house. There was no way we could afford to pay to have it done. We had to learn to do it ourselves.

Writer: How did you go about learning?

Rudy: I decided to go to a vocational school at night so that I could learn cabinetmaking and electrical wiring. Later Irene went so that she could study plumbing and general carpentry too.

Writer: Tell me about the kind of changes you made to the house.

Irene: You know, you never realize the problems disabled people have until it affects your own family. Nowadays most public buildings have ramps so that people in wheelchairs can get in, and buses have lifts so that people with disabilities can get on and off. But just imagine the problems Paul would have in your house. We needed wide halls so that he could move from one room to another. And we needed a big bathroom so that he could be as independent as possible. We had to change a lot.

Writer: Where did you start?

Irene: The electrical system. Rudy completely rewired the house so that Paul could turn on and off the lights and plug in appliances. We had to redo the whole house so that Paul could reach things and do what he wanted.

Writer: What are you working on now?

Irene: We've just finished redoing the kitchen so that Paul can do a little cooking. Now we're converting the garage into a workshop so that he can make some money fixing appliances.

Writer: How do you plan to spend the $50,000 prize?

Irene: We're hoping to start our own construction business so that we can do conversions for people with disabilities.

Look at this:

I did this so that	he she	could couldn't	do that.
	this that	would wouldn't	happen.

I'm doing this I do this	so that	he she	can can't	do that.
		this that	will won't	happen.

or

So that	he she	could couldn't	do that,	I did this.
	this that	would wouldn't	happen,	

So that	he she	can can't	do that,	I'm doing this.
	this that	will won't	happen,	I do this.

Exercise 1

These are some of the things the Ciprianis did. Look at the chart, ask questions with *Why?* and *What's the purpose of…?*, and answer them.

IMPROVEMENT	PURPOSE
put in swinging doors	Paul could push through with his wheelchair.
widen doors	The wheelchair could get through.
install phones in every room	Paul could always get to one.
lower light switches	Paul could reach them.
put in ramps	The wheelchair could get in and out.
design remote control device	Paul could open and close the front door.

Exercise 2

Here are some of the things the Ciprianis are going to do. Ask questions and answer them.

PLAN	PURPOSE
install an elevator	He'll be able to get upstairs on his own.
convert garage into workshop	He'll be able to make some money.
install lift on van	The wheelchair will be able to get in and out.
design a beeper system	He can call us at any time.

Exercise 3

Discuss: Have you ever changed anything in your home? Why?

Construction Technologies International, Inc.

To: Danga River Irrigation Project employees
From: William Moore, Project Director
Re: Advice to employees going to Mandanga

Medical precautions

1. To avoid infection, have your doctor give you shots for typhoid, cholera and yellow fever before departure.

2. To prevent malaria, start taking Aralan tablets two weeks before departure.

3. To prevent heat exhaustion, be sure to drink adequate quantities of liquids.

4. Take salt tablets to avoid getting dehydrated.

5. Limit the time you spend working in direct sunlight in order to prevent sunstroke.

Local customs

1. Avoid wearing shorts or bathing suits in religious buildings.

2. Remove your shoes before entering private homes to avoid offending your host.

3. Avoid wearing bikinis or other revealing bathing suits.

Useful expressions

In order not to appear rude, learn a few expressions in Mandangan before your arrival there:

Mandangan	English
Bonday.	Hello.
Lay tah.	Good-bye.
Yep.	Yes.
Naw.	No.
Ah bruh cuh dah bruh.	Please.
Muh chah bliged.	Thank you.
Kul.	You're welcome.
Oop zee.	Excuse me.
Up leh zur.	It's nice to see you.
Hi dee du?	How are you?
Oh key doe key.	Fine.
Wah chow!	Be careful!

Exercise 1

Look at the expressions in Mandangan. Practice with a partner using: *How do you say (this) in Mandangan? Can you translate (this) into Mandangan? What does (that) mean in English?*

Look at this:

| Do this | so that you don't | do that. |
| | in order not to | |

Do this	to	avoid	that.
	in order to		doing that.
	so that you can		

Do this	to prevent	that (from happening).
	to stop	something (from) happening.
	to keep	somebody (from) doing that.

Exercise 2

Why should we keep plastic bags away from babies?

To avoid the danger of suffocation.
or
To prevent babies from suffocating (themselves).

Look at the table above. Ask questions about these warning labels, and answer them.

CONTACT LENS CLEANER

To avoid contamination, do not touch tip of bottle to any surface.

Zeno Cassette Player
WARNING:
To prevent fire or shock hazard, do not expose this appliance to rain or moisture.

TEFL
Non-stick frying pan
Always use wooden or plastic utensils to avoid scratching.

TEXOIL Motor Oil
To prevent engine wear, always change oil at regular intervals.

WARNING
This is NOT a toy.
To avoid danger of suffocation, keep this plastic bag away from babies and young children.

A new way of life

Announcer: Tonight on *TV Close-up* our correspondent Diana Romero will talk to some "rat-race dropouts"—some very happy people who've given up regular jobs and high salaries to start a new way of life.

Diana: I'm here in northern Vermont, where the nearest town is more than 25 miles away. Dan and Michelle Gallagher were born and lived most of their lives in Boston. Dan was vice president of marketing for a publishing company, and Michelle was an advertising executive. They gave up their jobs and moved to this remote area of Vermont four years ago. Michelle, what made you give up everything for this?

Michelle: Everything? A big house and expensive cars aren't everything. We used to work long hours—such long hours, in fact, that we hardly ever saw each other. We wanted to do this years ago, but we were making so much money that we were afraid to quit our jobs. Even the time we spent at home was so hectic that we never had time to just be together. So four years ago we traveled around New England on vacation. We saw this place. It was for sale, and we liked it so much we decided to buy it. The next week we quit our jobs, sold most of our things, and here we are!

Diana: How do you earn a living?

Michelle: We don't need a lot. We have two milk cows and a few chickens. We grow all our own vegetables. It's a simple life. We're still so busy that we work from dawn to dark, but we're together. And now we have Kimberly, who's three. We're happier than we've ever been.

Diana: The motorcycle I'm standing next to is a very special one. Special because it's been all the way around the world. It belongs to Luke Musto, who has just come back here to Detroit after a three-year motorcycle trip. Luke, what led you to quit your job and make this trip?

Luke: I worked in a car factory on the assembly line. I made good money, but it was really monotonous. It was so routine that I never had to think. My job is done by a robot now. Big surprise…. Anyway, I bought this bike secondhand, put two packs on the back, and got myself on a freighter to Europe.

Diana: What did you do for money?

Luke: I had a little money saved up, but of course it didn't last long. I had to find work where I could. I did a lot of different things— picked fruit, washed dishes, worked as a mechanic.

Diana: How did people react to you?

Luke: Everywhere I went, people were so friendly that I always felt right at home. There was such a tremendous amount of interest in the bike that it was easy to start a conversation. Usually, you can communicate without knowing the language.

Diana: Did you ever feel like giving up and coming home?

Luke: Only once, in Bangladesh. I got so sick from something I ate that I had to go to a hospital. But it didn't last long.

Diana: You've had such an exciting time that you'll find it hard to settle down in Detroit, won't you?

Luke: I'm not going to. Next week I'm leaving again, but this time I'm heading south—to Tierra del Fuego. See you when I get back!

Exercise 1

The people were very friendly. He felt welcome.
The people were so friendly that he felt welcome.

Continue.
1. He was very old. He couldn't walk.
2. She was very busy. She didn't stop for lunch.
3. She was very late. She missed the plane.
4. He was very sick. He couldn't go out.
5. She had spent too much money. She couldn't afford another trip.
6. There were too many people in the boat. It sank.

Exercise 2

The farm was so beautiful that they bought it.
It was such a beautiful farm that they bought it.

Continue.
1. The book was so interesting that she couldn't stop reading it.
2. The problems were so hard that nobody could solve them.
3. The doctor was so friendly that everybody liked her.
4. The box was so heavy that he couldn't lift it.
5. The trip was so exciting that he's going again.

Exercise 3

She was such a good tennis player that nobody ever beat her.
The tennis player was so good that nobody ever beat her.

Continue.
1. It was such a dangerous job that nobody would do it.
2. He was such a good dancer that he won the prize.
3. They were such boring programs that nobody watched them.
4. It was such a crazy story that nobody believed it.

Exercise 4

Discuss: Would you ever consider being a "rat-race dropout?"

At 7:20 PM on May 6, 1937, the world's largest airship, the *Hindenburg*, floated majestically over Lakehurst Airport, New Jersey, after an uneventful crossing from Frankfurt, Germany. There were 97 people on board for the first Atlantic crossing of the season. There were a number of reporters waiting to greet it. Suddenly radio listeners heard the commentator screaming, "Oh, my God! It's broken into flames. It's flashing…flashing. It's flashing terribly." Thirty-two seconds later the airship had disintegrated and 35 people were dead. The Age of the Airship was over.

The *Hindenburg* was the last in a series of airships which had been developed over 40 years in both Europe and the United States. They were designed to carry passengers and cargo over long distances. The *Hindenburg* could carry 50 passengers in 25 luxury cabins with all the amenities of a first-class hotel. All the cabins had hot and cold water and electric heating. There was a dining room, a bar, and a lounge with a dance floor and a baby grand piano. The *Hindenburg* had been built to rival the great luxury transatlantic liners—it was able to cross the Atlantic in less than half the time of a liner. By 1937 it had carried 1,000 passengers safely and had even transported circus animals and cars. Its sister ship, the *Graf Zeppelin,* had flown over a million miles (1.6 million km), and had carried 13,100 passengers without incident.

Nobody knows the exact cause of the *Hindenburg* disaster. The *Hindenburg* was filled with hydrogen, which is a highly flammable gas, and every safety precaution had been taken to prevent accidents. Sabotage has been suggested, but experts at the time believed that it was caused by leaking gas which was ignited by static electricity. It had been waiting to land for three hours because of heavy thunderstorms. The explosion happened just as the first mooring rope, which was wet, touched the ground. The most surprising thing is that 62 people managed to escape. The fatalities were highest among the crew members, many of whom were working deep inside the airship. After the *Hindenburg* disaster, all airships were grounded, and until recently, they have never been seriously considered as a commercial proposition.

Airships—Achievements and Disasters

1852	First airship flew over Paris.
1910–14	Five zeppelin airships operated commercial flights within Germany, carrying 35,000 people without injury.
1914–8	Military zeppelins took part in 53 bombing raids on London during the First World War.
1919	British "R34." First transatlantic crossing. Both directions (10,128 km in 183 hours).
1925	*U.S. Shenandoah* (first helium airship) destroyed in a storm over Ohio. Heavy loss of life.
1926	Italian airship, the *Norge,* flew over North Pole.
1929	German *Graf Zeppelin* flew around the world. Began commercial transatlantic flights.
1930	British "R101" crashed in France. Killed 42 out of 48 on board. British airship program canceled.
1931	*U.S. Akron* in service in USA—could carry 207 passengers.
1933	*Akron* wrecked in a storm.
1935	Sister ship, *U.S. Macon,* wrecked.
1936	*Hindenburg* built. Carried 117 passengers in one flight.
1937	*Hindenburg* crashed.
1938	*Graf Zeppelin II* completed.
1940	Both *Graf Zeppelins* scrapped.
1958	U.S. Navy built a radar airship, the "ZPG-3W."
1960	"ZPG-3W" crashed in the ocean.
1961	U.S. Navy airship program ended.
Present:	Currently airships (called *blimps)* are used to promote various corporations

Exercise 1

Match the words from the story in Column 1 with their synonyms in Column 2.

COLUMN 1	COLUMN 2
majestically	conveniences
uneventful	deaths
disintegrated	catastrophe
amenities	ordinary
rival	blast
transported	compete with
disaster	undertaking
ignited	broken up
explosion	grandly
fatalities	lighted
proposition	carried

Exercise 2

Discuss: Would you like to take a ride in a blimp? Why or why not?

Eating Out
by Mimi Hilton

The Blue Mill
133 West River St.
730-8375
Closed Monday.
Reservations recommended.

This 3-month-old restaurant has attracted attention because it is a restored, 150-year-old mill. The decor is charming and warm in an early-American country style.

The menu is also very American, though it is a bit too traditional for my taste. The most delicious main course we tried was the country stew, which consisted of potatoes, carrots, peas, mushrooms, very tender beef, and – surprise – some smoked pork sausage. Because top-quality beef was used, it was unusually good. Among other well-prepared main courses was the fried chicken, because it wasn't pre-cooked and then reheated.

Although the vegetables that came with the main courses were fresh, they were overcooked. The only exception was the string beans, which were green and crisp (a mistake?!).

Because the main courses are so large, there is really no need for an appetizer or soup. For those who want a light meal, however, I can recommend the green salad. The clam chowder was tasty because it was homemade, but it had no special distinction. The oysters on the half-shell were nicely served on a bed of ice, although I would have preferred a better sauce for them.

If you can still eat dessert after all this, plus some rather good homemade bread and creamery butter, try the apple pie. The apples were juicy and firm and the pastry was light.

Although service at this friendly restaurant is supposed to be good, don't count on it. Maybe because it was crowded each time we went, we found service to be very slow.

Diner's Journal

by Eric Miller

New Fast-Food Chain Arrives

The *Nashville Superburger* chain, which started in that Tennessee city six years ago, opened its first store here last month. I was interested to see the connection between Nashville, the capital of country music, and hamburgers. Would the burgers be Southern-fried? Would they be shaped like guitars? Well, I've been there twice and didn't find any real difference between Nashville Superburgers and any other large, impersonal fast-food chain.

Although there were long lines, service was incredibly fast. The menu is limited to a variety of hamburgers, all reasonably priced.

I had the "Super-Duperburger." Although the meat itself was rather bland and tasteless, the "secret relish" made it passable. The french fries, however, were the best I've ever eaten at a fast-food restaurant.

Although I usually shy away from milk shakes in fast-food places, I felt I should try one here, because everyone seemed to be drinking one. Nashville Superburger's milk shakes are supposed to be "healthier" than the competition, probably because there is not one natural ingredient in them. Even though they may be low in cholesterol, I prefer whole milk, real ice cream, and natural flavorings in my milk shakes, thank you.

Nashville Superburger is a sure bet when you're downtown and in a hurry. I was in and out in ten minutes. It reminded me of a highway filling station. But the fries are great!

Look at this:

It was raining. She took her umbrella.
She took her umbrella because it was raining.

It wasn't raining. He took his umbrella.
He took his umbrella | *although* | *it wasn't raining.*
                        | *though*
                        | *even though*

Exercise

Now combine these sentences with *because* or *although*.
1. He didn't take the job. The salary was good.
2. Sarah needed a new calculator. She bought one.
3. They're afraid of flying. They flew to New York.
4. Mark wasn't thirsty. He drank some milk.
5. They didn't buy the house. It was expensive.

Traveling on the Washington Metro presents few difficulties for visitors because of the clear color-coded map. At the bottom of the map you will find fare and travel-time information. You buy your farecard at one of the yellow vending machines. You can use nickels, dimes, quarters, one-dollar, five-dollar, ten-dollar, and twenty-dollar bills, and the machine will give you change. You have to use your farecard to enter the Metro system by inserting it into the slot at the gate. It will be returned to you at the other side of the gate. Do the same thing when exiting the system.

Listen to these people talking about the Metro map, and follow their routes on the map.

PIERO AND MARGHERITA HAVE JUST ARRIVED AT NATIONAL AIRPORT.

Piero: OK. We have to get to Deanwood. Can you see it?

Margherita: Yes, it's up here. It looks so easy. We just take the Yellow Line to L'Enfant Plaza, then change to the Orange Line. It goes straight there. It's the seventh stop from L'Enfant Plaza.

BETSY IS AT THE INFORMATION BOOTH AT THE PENTAGON.

Betsy: Excuse me. How do I get to Connecticut Avenue and Q Street? I mean, which is the nearest Metro station?

Attendant: You want Dupont Circle. Take a look at the map. You take the Yellow Line to Gallery Place. Then you'll have to change for the Red Line. It's the third stop.

Betsy: I see.

Attendant: Or you could take the Blue Line to Metro Center and change to the Red Line there.

Betsy: Which way is faster?

Attendant: It's about the same.

Betsy: Well, thank you.

🎧 Listening 1

Listen. Alice and Fred are at the Capitol Heights station. They're discussing two routes. Which one did they decide to take?

🎧 Listening 2

Listen. Alice and Fred are going to visit the Washington Monument. What station are they going to?

Exercise 1

Practice with a partner. Give directions from:
1. Court House to National Airport
2. Federal Triangle to Union Station
3. Potomac Avenue to Gallery Place
4. Dupont Circle to Rosslyn
5. Union Station to Arlington Cemetery
6. College Park to Court House

Exercise 2

Here are some famous Washington, DC landmarks with their nearest Metro stations. Make conversations about getting to them from: (a) Deanwood, (b) National Airport, and (c) Union Station.
1. The FBI–Federal Bureau of Investigation (Metro Center)
2. The Kennedy Center (Foggy Bottom-GWU)
3. The Washington Monument (Smithsonian)
4. The National Air and Space Museum (L'Enfant Plaza)
5. The RFK Stadium (Stadium-Armory)

Exercise 3

Practice with a partner. State a departure point and destination. Your partner has to give you directions.

The Six O'Clock News

And now, the Six O'Clock Report with Jack Dennehy.

Good evening. Thousands of Portstown residents marched on City Hall today to protest plans to build a state prison near the city. Although a light rain was falling, an estimated 5,000 people marched over a mile from Portstown High School to City Hall, where Governor Brown and Mayor Henry Flores were meeting to discuss the project. A new prison is needed because the other state prisons are overcrowded. Several sites for the new prison were considered, but Portstown was chosen because, in the governor's words, "All areas in the state must share the problems of our prison system." Although the protesters asked to meet with the governor, he refused and returned to the capital. After the governor's departure, however, the mayor met with the organizers of the march and explained his position.

Four entire city blocks were evacuated this afternoon in Oceanside because of a gas explosion. The explosion occurred at 1:20 PM in a deserted building on Second Street. Fire Department officials believe that the explosion was due to leaking gas. The building had been empty for several months, and they suspect that a gas main had cracked because of vibrations from work being carried out by the city on the street.

Coast Guard helicopters went into action today after a yacht capsized in Coolidge Sound. Despite rain and high seas, the helicopters were able to rescue all but one of those aboard. Two men and two women were pulled to safety, but one of the men was pronounced dead on arrival despite the rescue team's efforts. The other three are in satisfactory condition. The fifth passenger, a woman, was not found. Although the Coast Guard continues its search, she is presumed drowned. The Coast Guard had issued a small-craft warning this morning, but the yacht set out from the Newgate Marina in spite of the warnings.

Incomplete reports have reached this station about a 100-mile-an-hour car chase on Portstown streets. Only minutes ago, according to these reports, Portstown police were alerted by an anonymous phone call and rushed to catch a gang that was breaking into a local discount clothing store. However, the gang of young males escaped in a late-model car that allegedly had been stolen two days ago in Harbor City. The gang was armed and fired several times at the police cars behind them. Nevertheless, the police were able to run the gang's car off the road and arrest all the members with no injuries on either side.

Now to sports: Portstown High School Stadium was filled last night when the Portstown Pirates played their traditional rivals, the Harbor City Raiders. Pirate quarterback Tony Rizzuto scored two touchdowns in the first half. Although the Raiders didn't score at all in the first half, they went on to win with two touchdowns and a field goal in the second half. In spite of the Pirates' good showing in the first half, they couldn't seem to do anything right in the second. The final score: Raiders 17, Pirates 14.

Look at this:

It was snowing, so they canceled the game.

or

They canceled the game	because it was snowing.
	because of	the snow.
	due to	

or

Because it was snowing,	they canceled the game.
Because of	the snow,	
Due to		

It was snowing, but they didn't cancel the game.

or

They didn't cancel the game	although it was snowing.
	in spite of	the snow.
	despite	

or

Although it was snowing,	they didn't cancel the game.
In spite of	the snow,	
Despite		

It was hard, but she managed to win.

or

| It was hard. | However, | she managed to win. |
| | Nevertheless, | |

or

| It was hard. | She managed to win, | however. |
| | | nevertheless. |

or

| It was hard. She managed, | however, | to win. |
| | nevertheless, | |

Exercise

Write one news item for your local area.

THE BRIDGEPORT TIMES

Thursday, January 1

Our New Year's Present to the President

Farmers bring in record soybean harvest this year

The president, speaking at the American Bar Association convention this year, asked why newpapers only print bad news. "Why don't they tell us things like how many planes landed safely in the United States in one day?" he asked. Here is our New Year's present to the president—a column of good-news items.

• In 1931, Alice Hoover Meyers, now 88 years old, began writing her first novel, about life in a small Kansas town. Last week, Milburn University Press published the 1,500-page novel, *The Women in the Club*, more than 60 years after Mrs. Meyers put pen to paper. When asked about her reaction to becoming a published author at age 88, Mrs. Meyers replied, "I hope there's time to write the next one!"

• O'Hare Airport in Chicago, the busiest airport in the United States, reports that a total of 645,586 planes took off and landed without incident during the year.

• Eleven Korean children with congenital heart defects, flown to the United States under the auspices of the American Medical Association, were successfully operated on last week at Houston General Hospital in Texas. After a brief convalescence, they will be flown back to Seoul. The AMA, which is sponsoring the "Big Heart" program, plans to help many other children from all over the world.

• The governor of California announced last week at a meeting of 200 state legislators that the state treasury has a surplus of over $200 million with nearly $1 billion projected for next year. This is an amazing accomplishment in view of the condition of thestate treasury six months ago–a $1.5 million deficit!

• According to reports, there were 2,439,000 civil and religious marriage ceremonies this year, an increase of 1% over the total for last year.

• Even farmers are smiling—that is, the soybean farmers, who were able to bring in a record harvest last year with a minimum effort—over 2 1/4 billion bushels.

• It was a great year for animals, too. Some residents of Bolton, Massachusetts, wanted to limit the number of pigs per farm, claiming that pigs depressed property values. A vote was taken, and the pig supporters won 305 to 195 not to restrict the number of porcine farm residents.

• CompTrac, a small Delaware construction company in business for less than a decade, was awarded a $40 million contract to build three schools in Kuwait. Winning large contracts seems to be a new trend for small businesses.

• The battle to clean up the West River is being won. Species of fish which even ten years ago could not have survived in the polluted water are being caught in increasing numbers.

• And a final note, The death rate from suicide is on the decline.

The company picnic

Every year, the Austin, Texas, operation of Lemon Computers gives a Fourth of July picnic for all its employees and their families. The picnic is held at a lake near town, and everyone enjoys swimming, water skiing, boating, playing games, and especially, eating the big barbecue lunch.

Leslie Carbone works in the Accounting Department. She's talking to Diane Romberg, the personnel director.
Leslie: Hi, Diane. Was that your son David you were just talking to?
Diane: Oh, hi, Leslie. Yeah, that was David. I don't know what to do with him. He never wants to play with the other kids.
Leslie: He certainly has grown since last year.
Diane: Yeah, he's much taller than most kids his age. Oh, well. How do you like the picnic? Are you having a good time?

Leslie: Oh, yes, great! I…uh… wanted to ask you about that job in the New York office.
Diane: It's definitely opening up. Are you still interested in it?
Leslie: I might be. I really don't know what to do. I'm really happy here in Austin, but it would be nice to be in New York. My family lives in New Jersey. Maybe I'll apply for it.
Diane: Why not? Drop by my office next week and I'll tell you what I can about it. Of course, you have to decide what you want.

Jackie Pulido is in charge of the Marketing Department. She's just seen Bart Conners, who works in the Advertising Department.
Bart: Jackie! I see you're back from your trip.
Jackie: Yes, I got in last night.
Bart: How did it go?

Jackie: Fabulous. What I saw over there really surprised me. I think there'll be a lot of demand for our new C2L personal computer.
Bart: That's very interesting.
Jackie: Yes, really. What I found was very encouraging. We have just what they're looking for.

Richard Eng is the Lemon Computers vice president who is in charge of the Austin operation. He's just run into Bob Ewing, who is the plant manager.
Richard: Hi, Bob. It's another good picnic, isn't it?
Bob: Yeah, it really is.
Richard: Did you get my memo about the meeting Wednesday?
Bob: Yeah, ten o'clock, right? Your memo didn't say what the meeting's about. It's not bad news, is it?
Richard: No, don't worry. It's good news in fact. What we need to do is increase production of the C2L. Either we'll have to go into overtime or we'll have to hire new people.
Bob: Terrific! What we'll have to look at is how much each way will cost.
Richard: Right, but we can cover the facts and figures on Wednesday. Let's not talk shop today. That's not what we're here for.
Bob: You're right. Have you tried the barbecued ribs?

Look at this:
I don't know *what* to do with him.
That's not *what* we're here for.
What I saw surprised me.

Exercise 1

Role play in groups. Each member of the group takes the role of one of the characters. First act out the conversations. Then improvise conversations as you circulate among the other characters at the picnic (for example, Diane Romberg and Jackie Pulido, Richard Eng and Bart Conners).

Exercise 2

Discuss: Are company-sponsored activities outside of work a good place to conduct business? Why or why not?

It's Alan Newman's first day on his first job. It's in the maintenance department of a large factory. Burt Hogg, who has worked there for 25 years, is showing Alan around.

Burt: All right, son. Any questions?
Alan: Uh…yeah. Where can I leave my jacket and things?
Burt: There's a row of lockers over there. It doesn't matter which one you use. Take whichever one you want.
Alan: Oh, thanks. And I have my Social Security card. They told me to bring it. Who should I show it to?
Burt: Just take it up to Personnel. You can show it to whoever is there.
Alan: When can I do that?
Burt: It really doesn't matter. Go whenever you want to, whenever it's convenient.
Alan: OK.

Alan: Oh, another thing, Burt. Where can I park my motorcycle?
Burt: There's plenty of room in the parking lot. Just don't put it in a space that's reserved. Other than that, you can leave it wherever there's room. Come on, I'll show you where you'll be working. In here. That's your workbench, and your stool is here. Just watch me at first and do whatever I tell you, OK?
Alan: OK.
Burt: First of all, you can clean these tools. There's some solvent in that bottle on the shelf.
Alan: All right. Is there any special way to do it?
Burt: Huh? A special way? No, Alan. Clean them however you want to. There's no special way.

10:30

Burt: Come on, Alan, you can stop for a while. It's time for a break.
Alan: Thanks.
Burt: Don't thank me, son. You're doing a good job. It's time for a cup of coffee—or whatever you want. Oh, and after the break, I want you to go to the supply room and get me a few things, OK?
Alan: Sure.
Burt: Good. I need a can of striped paint, a rubber hammer and a glass nail, a left-handed screwdriver, and a bucket of steam. Just tell them Burt sent you.

AT THE SUPPLY ROOM

Alan: Hi there.
Supply Clerk: Hi there.
Alan: I'm here to get a can of striped paint.
Supply Clerk: A what? What are you talking about?
Alan: I was sent here to pick up a can of striped paint.
Supply Clerk: And what wise guy told you to do that?
Alan: Burt—Burt Hogg.

Supply Clerk: Oh, Burt Hogg. I see. What color stripes would you like?
Alan: Oh. I don't know. Maybe I'd better ask him.
Supply Clerk: I suppose he told you to get a right-handed screwdriver too.
Alan: No, he wants a left-handed one.
Supply Clerk: Think about what you're saying. Just stop and think.
Alan: But Burt said…. Oh. Hmmm. Oh, yeah…uh…excuse me.

A FEW MINUTES LATER

Burt: What took you so long, Alan?
Alan: Well, the supply room didn't have what you wanted, so I filled out a requisition form and took it to the president's office. You've been here so long that I'm sure he'll approve whatever you need.

Exercise 1

A: What would you like to do tonight?
B: *I don't care—whatever you like.*

Continue.
1. Well, where would you like to go?
2. How do you want to go there?
3. Which would you rather take—a bus or a taxi?
4. When do you think we should leave?
5. Where do you want to go for dinner?
6. What do you want to have?
7. Who should we invite to the party?
8. What should we serve?

Exercise 2

A: What should I do with these old newspapers?
B: *It doesn't matter. Do whatever you want to.*

Continue.
1. So, which of these books can I borrow?
2. Who should I give my ticket to?
3. When can I come to see you?
4. How should I do it?
5. Where can I park my car?

Newspapers and magazines are full of advertisements that try to persuade people to change their appearance in one way or another. Look at these ads and discuss them.

ADVERTISEMENTS

NORTHEAST MAGAZINE

EARS PIERCED FOR FREE

With purchase of only one pair of our wide selection of studs and earrings.
No appointment necessary.
Also, nose piercing by appointment.

EASTERN JEWELRY CENTER

North Plaza Mall • Downtown West Haven • Southgate Mall • The Galleria

BE TALLER

with our custom-made shoes. We can add up to 2 inches to your height...and only *you* will ever know. Our unique design provides both comfort and confidence. Call for our free catalog today!

800-GET TALL

SPARTA
HEALTH AND FITNESS CENTER

Fully equipped gym • Latest equipment • Personal trainers
Sauna • Aerobic and Step classes • Solarium • Massage

L.B. of Scranton, PA, writes:
"I lost 20 pounds in 12 weeks. I feel younger, fitter, and happier … and I owe it all to the Sparta Center. I am a new woman…"

SPARTA HEALTH AND FITNESS CENTERS
In cities and towns throughout the country.
Check your white pages or call
(800) 675-9987 for the location nearest you.

"Anywhere, any size!"
LEO REMBRANDT
TATTOO ARTIST

Choose from a wide selection of designs and patterns. All kinds of lettering. Variety of colors. Quick, hygienic, almost painless method (electric needle). Non-toxic dyes.
210 Waterbury Road, Waterbury, NY 10767

"WOULD YOU LIKE A BODY LIKE MINE?"

I used to weigh 110 pounds until I discovered the Dynomatic™ System of bodybuilding. Three years later I became "Mr. Galaxy." Do yourself a favor.

Write now to:
Ed Sampson's Dynomatic System
P.O Box 40, Gotham, CA 91491

Bald? Balding? Receding Hairline?
Bald patches? Premature hair loss? Graying?

BEFORE

**Look years younger!
Contact the Brynner Hair Advisory Center**

AFTER

Call and arrange for an immediate free consultation. Completely confidential.
Lincoln Plaza, Fall River, MA 01234 Tel. (617) 588-0921

Skinner Surgical Institute

Cosmetic surgery by internationally famous plastic surgeon. Restore your youth, good looks, and self-confidence.

•Unsightly scars and lines removed
•Reshaping: nose, eyelids, jawlines, cheeks, lips
•Facelifts •Liposuction

Our clients have included leading figures from the worlds of entertainment, politics, and business. Please contact:

Skinner Surgical Institute
Box OUP, New York, NY 10017

THROW AWAY YOUR GLASSES AND CONTACT LENSES!

**Optical laser surgery IS HERE!
The new, painless option for better vision.
Call and ask for our video. No obligation.
Or come in for a free consultation.**

800-SEE-WELL

Hartford Eye Associates • 2987 Manchester Road • Suite 540 • Hartford , CT 06543

Visual gossip

Do you like reading about famous people? Have you ever seen a newspaper photograph of a celebrity in an embarrassing situation? Sometimes newspaper photos cause major scandals and can change lives. Leaders resign and governments fall after tabloid scandals, and we can't get enough of them.

Photographers (or *paparazzi*) will do almost anything to get the pictures that they sell to newspapers and magazines. They may rent helicopters, hot-air balloons, or even mini-submarines. They may stay out all night in freezing rain. They may get punched or even shot at. While they don't generally break the law, they may bribe doormen or security guards to get their shots.

🎧 Listening

Listen and match the celebrities with their picture. Take notes under each photograph.

Name: *Duchess of Lichtenburg*
Age: *37*
Occupation: *Duchess/multi-millionaire*
News: *Planning a secret wedding to limo driver.*

Name: . . .
Age: . . .
Occupation: . . .
News: . . .
. . .
. . .
. . .

Name: . . .
Age: . . .
Occupation: . . .
News: . . .
. . .
. . .
. . .

Name: . . .
Age: . . .
Occupation: . . .
News: . . .
. . .
. . .
. . .

Name: . . .
Age: . . .
Occupation: . . .
News: . . .
. . .
. . .
. . .

Name: . . .
Age: . . .
Occupation: . . .
News: . . .
. . .
. . .
. . .

Exercise

Discuss: Do celebrities have the right to private lives?

Our planet Earth is one of nine planets revolving around the Sun, a fairly small and ordinary star, which lies in the outer areas of the Milky Way galaxy. There are about 250 billion stars in our galaxy and billions of galaxies in the universe. People have always wondered about the possibility of intelligent life forms on other planets. In recent years this has become serious scientific speculation. Some scientists believe that there must be large numbers of stars with planets that could support living intelligent beings. Perhaps we will never know. The nearest star is 4.3 light-years away. A light-year is the distance covered by light [traveling at about 186,000 miles (300,000 kilometers) a second] in one year. It would take the fastest Earth spacecraft about 40,000 years to reach the nearest star.

For a number of years radio telescopes have been trying to pick up signals from outer space, so far without success. There are, however, millions of possible radio frequencies, and there is no reason why a completely alien civilization should not use a different type of communication, such as x rays or even a type of wave we have not yet discovered. Suppose contact were made with beings 300 light-years away. By the time we had sent our reply and received their response, the earth would be 600 years older. It would be an interesting, but rather slow-moving, conversation!

PIONEER 10

The first man-made object to leave our solar system was the *Pioneer 10* spacecraft. It was launched from Cape Kennedy on March 2, 1972. It was designed to pass close to the planet Jupiter. In 1983 it left the outer limits of the planetary system. A gold

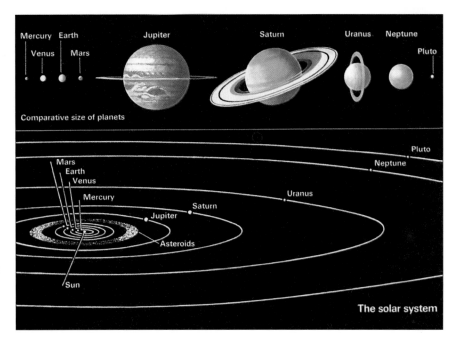

Comparative size of planets

The solar system

plaque, 6 inches by 9 inches (15.2 cm x 22.9 cm), was placed on the spacecraft. On the plaque is a diagram showing the solar system and its location in the galaxy. There is also a drawing of a man and a woman, standing in front of a picture of the spacecraft. The man's right hand is raised in a gesture of friendship. It is unlikely, however, that the plaque will ever be seen again. If it were found by an alien civilization, it seems improbable that they would be able to interpret it.

THE VOYAGER MISSION

Every 175 years the large outer planets—Jupiter, Saturn, Uranus, and Neptune—are in such a position that a spacecraft from Earth can fly past all of them. The two *Voyager* spacecrafts were launched in 1977 to photograph and investigate these planets. *Voyager 1* reached Jupiter in February 1979, and Saturn in November 1980. It sent back dramatic

pictures of the rings of Saturn and discovered previously unknown moons. It then left the solar system. *Voyager 2* reached Jupiter in July 1979, Saturn in August 1981, Uranus in January 1986, and Neptune in August 1989, before leaving the solar system to travel silently through space. Its next stop—no one knows.

As well as a pictorial plaque, *Voyager 2* carries a gold-sprayed disc. The disc contains greetings in 60 languages, 140 photographs, and one and a half hours of music and songs, ranging in style from Beethoven and Mozart to the Beatles and Chuck Berry.

Exercise 1

Imagine you could send a package, weighing up to 25 kilos, which could give an impression of civilization on Earth. This would include recordings, videotapes, photographs, film, etc. What would you choose to send and why?

Exercise 2

Space research costs billions of dollars. Some people think that the money would be better spent on more practical projects here on Earth. What do you think?

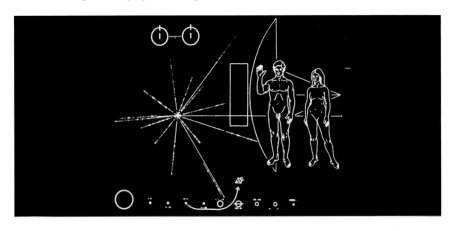

Janet and Bruce live in Houston. Janet's younger sister, Pam, who lives in Denver, is flying down to spend a long weekend with them.

Janet: Bruce, I think it's time to go and meet Pam at the airport.

Bruce: Oh, no, there's no need to hurry. There's plenty of time. It's only 8:30. There won't be much traffic at this time of night.

Janet: You never know, and I think your watch must be slow. I have 8:40. I'd rather be too early than too late!

Bruce: It'll take her a while to get her luggage.

Janet: Oh, come on, Bruce! It's time we were leaving. We can always have some coffee at the airport.

Bruce: I'd rather see the end of the basketball game, but never mind, we'd better go.

Bruce: Janet! Wait a minute. The phone's ringing.

Janet: Hello? Oh, Pam! Where are you?

Pam: I'm still in Denver. The flight's been delayed.

Janet: You caught us just in time.

Pam: Oh, good. The plane won't be leaving for another hour at least. Look, don't bother to come out to the airport.

Janet: It's no trouble. We'll meet you.

Pam: No, I'd really rather you didn't. Honestly.

Janet: Now, don't be silly, Pam. We'll pick you up.

Pam: No, Janet, I'd rather get a taxi.

Janet: We'll be there, Pam! See you later.

Janet: Oh, Bruce, there she is!

Bruce: It's about time.

Pam: Janet! Bruce! Mmm. It's wonderful to see you, but I'm really embarrassed. It's almost 12:30.

Janet: Well, we couldn't let you find your own way—not at this time of night.

Bruce: Do we have to wait for the luggage or is that all you have?

Pam: No, this is it. I didn't check anything.

Bruce: Great! It always takes forever at this airport.

Janet: I know. It's about time they did something about it.

Bruce: I'll go and get the car. I won't be long.

Janet: Well, Pam, what would you rather do tomorrow morning, sleep in or go shopping?

Pam: You mean this morning! I'd rather go shopping, but there's no need for you to come with me. I'd rather you slept in. You must be exhausted! Besides, it isn't as if this were my first visit to Houston.

Look at this:

I'd rather	go there.	

I'd rather	you	went there.
	he	didn't go there.
	she	
	we	
	they	

It's (about) time	to go.
	we left.
	we were leaving.

It isn't as	if	this were my first visit.
	though	he didn't know.

Exercise 1

The baggage handling is slow. They should do something about it.
It's about time they did something about it.

Continue.
1. It's late. We should go to the airport.
2. She's getting tired. She should go to bed.
3. He coughs a lot. He should stop smoking.
4. The windows are dirty. We should clean them.
5. The bus is late. It should be here.
6. He's bored. He should find an interesting job.

Exercise 2

Are you going to do it?
No, I'd rather not do it. I'd rather you did it.

Continue.
1. Are you going to write to her?
2. Would you like to drive?
3. Do you want to ask him?
4. Would you like to choose?
5. Do you want to arrange it?
6. Are you going to see the manager?

Beat it. This is private!

Thank God you got here, officer. The driver's losing blood fast.

I've been mugged!

Officer, I did not go through a red light.

They took all the money in the cash register.

She's only three years old, and she's been missing for two hours.

"Thanks for inviting me to speak at your career assembly. You've asked me to talk about what it's like being a police officer. Well, I'm going to be honest with you. It's no picnic being a police officer in New York and you have to be sure it's what you really want to do. When people need your help, they're only too happy to see you. But show up when they don't want you and what you can get called isn't fit to print. You arrive for work and have no idea what the day will bring: a traffic accident or a murder, an armed robbery or a false alarm, a request for directions or a drug overdose. I get asked about treatment for sick canaries, Social Security payments, politics, and prison visits. I have to deal with family conflicts. I get anonymous threatening letters and phone calls—and a lot of times I recognize who they're from. I rarely complete a holiday shift, especially Christmas, without having to report a suicide, usually caused by loneliness. Every day there are drunks, fights, bodies, demonstrations, the brutal and the brave, the villains and the victims, the haters and the lovers, and the just plain indifferent. It isn't easy.

What kind of person measures up to such a job? Any one of you. There's no minimum height requirement—you can be tall or short. But regardless of your height, you're obviously no good if you don't have the stature for the job. This means having concern for people, a real sense of fair play, and common sense. And if you don't have a sense of humor, forget it. These qualities are more important than qualifications, although you need some of those too. You have to be a high school graduate and at least 20 years old to get into the Police Academy. And those exams are tough. First you have to pass a written exam. If you make it through that, you have to take a physical exam, and you'd better be in good shape. If you pass that, you go to the Police Academy for six months.

Now, the pay starts at about $26,000 a year. And believe me, you'll earn every penny of it. You'll have to put up with lonely hours on the night shift and you'll probably work every Christmas. But the rewards you can get for doing a good job will more than compensate for the low pay. If I haven't dimmed your enthusiasm and you're still interested, you can do two things. First read a few books written by ex-cops. They'll tell you plenty. And also get in touch with the Department of Personnel, 55 Thomas Street, New York, NY. Or call them at (212) 566-8790. They'll tell you when the next exam is being given.

Thanks a lot. And good luck."

Exercise 1

Answer these questions.
1. Who do you think the speaker is?
2. What do you think the speaker means by the following:
   a. "I'm going to be honest with you."
   b. "It's no picnic being a police officer."
   c. "What you can get called isn't fit to print."
3. What's a typical day like for a New York City police officer?
4. What qualities are needed by someone who wants to become a police officer?
5. What are the age and education requirements for entrance into the Police Academy?
6. What steps does a person have to take to become a police officer?
7. What two things should someone do if he or she is interested in becoming a police officer?

Exercise 2

Discuss: A lot of television shows and movies take place in New York City. Why do you think this is? Have you been to New York? Would you like to go? Why or why not?

The microchip revolution

When computers were first used, one computer filled an entire room. But then, in 1948, the transistor was invented by three Bell Laboratories scientists, and the computer was transformed from a huge, unreliable, heat-producing machine into a smaller, more dependable, cooler one. New products were designed using this new technology. But a problem developed: As the parts going into products became smaller, wiring them together became an almost impossible job. Computers of that time typically had more than 20,000 transistors and thousands of other components.

In 1958, two different men at two different American companies separately developed a model of a circuit that was built on a small piece of silicon. There followed a dispute over patent rights, but the dispute was eventually settled. Both men are now considered co-inventors of one of the greatest technological ideas of our time, the chip.

The chip—also called microchip and integrated circuit—is a tiny piece of silicon around 1 cm square. It is densely packed with miniature electronic components. The components are integrated with each other to perform control, logic, and memory functions. They require very little power and perform their functions well.

Given the fact that the average chip is smaller than a thumbnail and may contain millions of components, it is remarkable that it can be manufactured. In fact, manufacturing proved to be so difficult that it wasn't until two years after the chip was created that the first chips were available for sale.

Nowadays, we take for granted all the things that can be done because of the development of the chip. Chips are used in cars to make sure the fuel mixture is correct. They are used in cameras, calculators, and watches to operate their main functions. In the medical field, chips are used in pacemakers, hearing aids, and almost every other medical device of any complexity. Chips are installed in household appliances, such as refrigerators, washer-dryers, microwave ovens, TV sets, VCRs, stereos, alarm systems, and telephones. In some cases, they perform functions that once had to be performed manually. In other cases, they perform new functions, such as timing a telephone call, that were not available before. Of course, chips are the building blocks of most computers, and they enable us to have computers on our desks that do the kinds of operations once reserved for computers that filled entire rooms.

Look at this:

New products *were designed* using the new computer technology.

Both men *are* now *considered* co-inventors of one of the greatest technological ideas of our time, the chip.

Nowadays, we take for granted all the things that *can be done* because of the development of the chip.

In some cases, they perform functions that once *had to be performed* manually.

Exercise

Three Bell Laboratories scientists *invented* the transistor.
The transistor was invented by three Bell Laboratories scientists.

Continue.
1. The invention of the transistor *transformed* the computer.
2. Two different men separately *developed* a model of a circuit.
3. They eventually *settled* a dispute over patent rights.
4. They *packed* the chip with miniature electronic components.
5. They *integrated* the components with each other to perform control, logic, and memory functions.
6. It is remarkable that they can *manufacture* the chip.
7. We now take for granted all the things we *can do* because of the chip.
8. Car manufacturers *use* chips to make sure the fuel mixture is correct.
9. Electronics manufacturers *use* chips in cameras, calculators, and watches to operate their main functions.
10. Chips allow machines to do things which they never *could do* before.

Gold rush

CALIFORNIA

In 1848, gold was discovered at Sutter's Mill, about 100 miles east of San Francisco, and the first great gold rush began. Within a year 100,000 people, only 8,000 of whom were women, had reached the coast of California. More than half of them had traveled overland across the American continent. "Gold fever" began to spread. Homes, farms, and stores were abandoned as everybody raced for California. Many came by sea, and in July 1850, more than 500 ships were anchored in San Francisco Bay, many of which had been deserted by gold-hungry sailors. A few people became fabulously rich, but it was a risky business. Law and order broke down. Even if a miner "struck it rich" there were always those who would try to take it away: gamblers, outlaws, thieves, and saloon keepers.

AUSTRALIA

The next major gold rush occurred in 1851, when gold was struck in New South Wales, Australia. This led to another stampede, and many rich finds were made. Other discoveries were made in Victoria and Kalgoorlie, Western Australia. In some places massive nuggets of gold were found accidentally, just lying on the ground. The "Welcome Stranger" nugget, which was found in 1869, weighed almost 173 pounds (78.47 kilos).

THE YUKON

Perhaps the most difficult conditions were experienced by those prospectors who braved the Canadian winters to win gold from the Yukon and Klondike rivers. On August 16, 1896, three prospectors struck gold in Bonanza Creek, a tributary of the Klondike River, and then in a second creek which was named *Eldorado*. In the Yukon, gold was obtained by washing gravel from riverbeds, and soon as much as $800 worth of gold was being taken from a single pay of dirt. Within a year, Dawson had grown from nothing to a town of 30,000 people. Everybody who entered the country had to carry a year's supply of food and mining equipment over steep and frozen mountain passes. Horses and donkeys died in the ice and snow, but the people kept on going. It is estimated that of the 100,000 people who set out for the Klondike, fewer than 40,000 actually arrived. Only 4,000 ever found gold, and very few of these became rich.

SOUTH AFRICA

By the turn of the century gold had been found in South Africa, and this laid the foundation for the world's largest gold-mining industry. Today South Africa accounts for 70% of world gold production. Vast sums of money are being invested, and modern mining technology is being used to squeeze gold from the rock.

TWENTIETH-CENTURY GOLD RUSH

New finds are being made in the former Soviet Union, Saudi Arabia, and the United States. The largest single mine in the world was discovered in Uzbekistan, then a Soviet republic, in 1958. However, in spite of recent finds, modern-day "gold rushes" are usually confined to speculation on the gold markets of Zurich, London, and New York. At times of economic uncertainty investors rush hysterically to buy gold, and the price soars, often only to fall back again. Gold fever is in many ways irrational, but historically gold has always held its value, and it is likely that in an uncertain world it will continue to do so.

Exercise 1

Match the words from the story in Column 1 with their meanings in Column 2.

COLUMN 1	COLUMN 2
nugget	a river or stream that flows into a larger one
stampede	
tributary	a narrow passage
gravel	a criminal
pass	a sudden rush of people or animals
outlaw	a small lump
	a mixture of small bits of rock or small stones

Exercise 2

Find words in the story that mean the same thing as the highlighted words.
1. The global economy is *unpredictable*.
2. They *roughly calculated* that only 40% of the people actually arrived in the Klondike.
3. Investors can make a lot of money if the price of gold *suddenly goes high*.
4. Only a small percentage of the miners actually *discovered* gold.
5. Prospectors in Canada *courageously faced* the cold and the ice.
6. Thinking that you're going to find gold is somewhat *unreasonable*.
7. New gold rushes are *limited* to trading gold in the world's gold markets.
8. Some prospectors found *huge* nuggets just lying around.
9. The ships were *abandoned* by the sailors, who went in search of gold.
10. Some investors have put *very large* amounts of money into mining for gold.

Exercise 3

Discuss: What would you do if gold was discovered near your home?

John: Good morning. This is *What's New, Portstown?*, Delaware's favorite radio talk show. I'm your host, John Barca. In the studio with me is Sandy Farnham, the daughter of famous circus owner T.P. Farnham. Sandy, the circus will be here in Portstown for two weeks. That's right, isn't it?

Sandy: Yes, that's right, John. We open tomorrow for two weeks.

John: Has the circus arrived yet, Sandy?

Sandy: No, not yet. It's on the road somewhere between New Jersey and here.

John: I suppose there's a lot to be done between now and the first show.

Sandy: Yes. I've already been here for three days. There were all the advance arrangements to be made. It's like preparing for a small invasion, I guess you could say.

John: What do you mean?

Sandy: Well, there are so many things to be done, you know. There are posters to be put up, newspaper ads to be arranged, local workers to be hired. It goes on and on.

John: When will the circus actually arrive?

Sandy: In the next hour or two. The first trucks should be arriving any minute now, and then the hard work really begins.

John: Most people love the circus. But not many realize how much work there is, do they?

Sandy: That's right. We'll be working all day and most of the night. It's a lot like moving a small army. But I'm keeping my fingers crossed. By tomorrow morning everything will have been set up in time for the afternoon performance. But first there's the big parade down Main Street at 11:30. Don't forget to come out and see us.

John: Thank you, Sandy, for coming in to talk to us. Now don't forget, folks. The big circus parade will start from the pier at 11:30, go along Main Street past the high school, and end in Lincoln Park. Farnham's Circus will be in town for two weeks, until August 28. Now for our next guest…

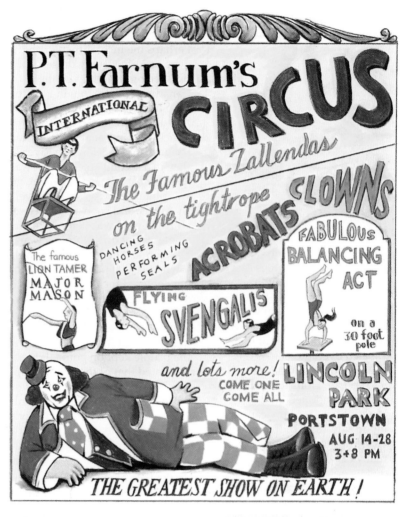

Exercise 1

This is Sandy's checklist of arrangements:
1. arrange telephone lines (Delaware Telephone Company)
2. consult police about parking (Portstown Police Department)
3. connect water supply (Portstown Department of Sanitation)
4. place ads (*Portstown Echo, Delaware Press*, Portstown radio station WPTD)
5. order food supplies for animals (Dover Feed Company)
6. arrange for fire protection (Portstown Fire Department)

All of these things will have been done before the circus arrives. Make sentences.
A telephone line will have been arranged. She'll have contacted the Delaware Telephone Company.

Exercise 2

Sandy's brother, Eddie Farnham, is in charge of the animals. This is his checklist:
1. unload animals
2. collect food supplies
3. clean cages
4. feed animals
5. check sanitary arrangements for the animals
6. provide straw for animals

Make sentences.
The animals have to be unloaded.

Exercise 3

It's eleven o'clock on Sunday morning. There's a lot to be done. Sandy's father, T.P. Farnham, is in charge of the arrangements.
1. erect big top
2. set up ticket office
3. park wagons
4. put up stands
5. erect cages
6. connect generators
7. put up safety net
8. set up tightrope
9. put up trapezes
10. set up bandstand
11. place loudspeakers in tent
12. connect amplifiers
13. set up and connect lights
14. connect microphones
15. check everything

Make sentences.
There's the big top to be erected.

Anne: Tim! That bathroom faucet is still dripping. It's driving me crazy! I thought you said you were going to fix it.

Tim: Oh, yeah. The washer needs replacing.

Anne: Why don't you replace it then?

Tim: That's easier said than done. I think you'd better call a plumber and get it done. I'm not really sure how to do it. Sorry, Mom.

Exercise 1

Make conversations using the following:

1. that light's still broken/socket/electrician
2. the brake lights on my car aren't working/bulb/take it to a garage
3. one of the burners on the stove isn't working/heating element/electrician
4. the reception on this TV set is very poor/cable/someone from the cable company

---

Mark and Tina are going on vacation next week. They're driving to Las Vegas. Mark always gives Tina a lift to work. He's dropping her off outside her office.

Mark: Tina, I won't be able to pick you up from work tonight. I'm having the car tuned up. I thought we'd better have it done before we go.

Tina: Good idea. When are you picking it up?

Mark: At a quarter to six. Why?

Tina: Well, I want to have my hair done before we leave. I'll try to make an appointment to get it done after work. Then you can pick me up at the hairdresser's.

Mark: OK. Call me at work and let me know what time, OK?

Tina: All right, I'll call you later. Bye.

Exercise 2

TIPS FOR VACATION DRIVERS

Before leaving on a long trip, don't forget to:
- have a complete tune-up
- change the oil
- check the battery
- test the brakes
- check the tires carefully and
- change or rotate if necessary

Mark doesn't have time to do any of these things himself.

He's going to have the car tuned up.

Make five more sentences.

Exercise 3

Tina's going to have her hair done.

Make sentences with:
wash/shampoo/trim/dye/cut/perm

Exercise 4

HOUSES FOR SALE

Quaint farmhouse. Built 1872. 3 bedrooms. Handyman's special. Needs work. Outdoor plumbing. Ideal for roughing it or for do-it-yourself enthusiast. Very reasonable price. Uciardi & Cotten Real Estate Agency, Concord. (603) 689-1242.

Look at the ad for a farmhouse in New Hampshire. It is old and in very bad condition. Imagine that you were interested in buying it. What do you think might need to be done to it?

The house might need repainting.

Make a list.

Listening 1

Listen to the conversation between a real estate agent and Robin and Gene Harvey, who are looking at the house. Check any items on your list that are mentioned in the conversation.

Listening 2

When Robin and Gene are talking about the house, they mention some things that they could do themselves and some things they would have to have done. Look at the chart below and the example: *They would have to have new cabinets and major appliances put in.* Listen to the conversation again and complete the chart.

	Do it themselves	Have it done by someone else
Put in new cabinets and major appliances		✔
Install plumbing for modern kitchen		
Put down new tiles on floor		
Rewire house		
Put in more electrical outlets		
Cover all walls with plasterboard		
Paint all walls and ceilings		
Convert small bedroom into bathroom		
Install bath and toilet plumbing		
Repair roof		
Put in new oil burner		
Weatherproof windows		
Put in insulation		

Honolulu Marathon: More Than 22,000 Will Hit the Road

Monday, December 10, 1994

More than 22,000 runners will compete in Honolulu's twenty-first annual marathon, which will kick off at 5:30 AM tomorrow. About 64% of the runners come from Japan, about 28% from Hawaii, 4% from the Mainland, and 3% from other foreign countries. A third of the competitors are women.

Kenya's Cosmas Ndeti, 23, is expected to take first place for the men. He should complete the 26 miles and 385 yards (add metric conversion) in about 2 hours, 10 minutes. The first place female winner is expected to be Holland's Carla Beurskens, 41, who will probably come in at about 2 hours, 30 minutes. A victory is worth $10,000 to each man and woman who places first, but the prize doubles if a record is set. Beurskens holds the women's record of 2:31:01. Ibrahim Hussein, also of Kenya,

holds the men's record of 2:11:43. Both set their records in 1986.

The marathon won't be a special occasion for just the winners. For Allan Katz, a radiologist from Largo, Florida, the marathon will be the perfect way to celebrate his fiftieth birthday. "When I heard the Honolulu Marathon was on my birthday," he said, "I just knew I had to be here. It's my thirty-third marathon, but by far, the most memorable." Dr. Katz expects to finish in about three and a half hours.

Questionnaire

1. Would you describe yourself as:
   ☐ Very fit ☐ Average
   ☐ Pretty fit ☐ Out of shape

2. Do you ever get out of breath?
   ☐ Yes ☐ No
   Can you touch your toes (without bending your knees)?
   ☐ Yes ☐ No
   Can you run for half a mile?
   ☐ Yes ☐ No
   Can you hang from a bar, supporting your own weight for 20 seconds?
   ☐ Yes ☐ No

3. Does your daily routine involve any physical exertion?
   ☐ Yes ☐ No

4. Do you exercise regularly?
   ☐ Yes ☐ No

5. If you exercise regularly, how often do you do it?
   ☐ Every day
   ☐ Every other day
   ☐ More than once a week
   ☐ Once a week
   ☐ Less than once a week

6. If you exercise regularly, what do you do?
   ☐ Sports ☐ Dancing ☐ Walking
   ☐ Jogging ☐ Bicycling ☐ Weightlifting
   ☐ Yoga ☐ Swimming
   ☐ Other (What other types?)
   _____

7. If you participate in sports, what is your favorite sport?
   ☐ Soccer ☐ American football
   ☐ Baseball ☐ Basketball
   ☐ Tennis ☐ Other (Specify)
   _____

8. Do you own any sports equipment?
   ☐ Yes ☐ No
   If so, what?
   _____

9. Do you/did you have to participate in sports at school/college?
   ☐ Yes ☐ No
   If so, which ones?
   _____
   How often?
   _____

10. Do you/did you have Phys. Ed. (Physical Education) classes at school/college?
    ☐ Yes ☐ No

11. Do you think sports or physical education should be a compulsory part of the school curriculum?
    ☐ Yes ☐ No

12. Why?/Why not?
    _____
    _____
    _____
    _____
    _____

Exercise 1

Using the questionnaire above, interview another student. Then switch roles, and answer your partner's questions about your exercise habits.

Here are instructions for two fitness exercises:

WARM-UP EXERCISE

Stand with feet apart and arms out at shoulder level. Bend forward, twisting the torso at the same time to touch the right hand to the left foot. Stand upright again with arms out. Then bend forward and twist, touching the left hand to the right foot. Repeat 10 times on each side the first day, gradually increasing to 20 repetitions on each side.

TWISTING SIT-UPS

Lie on your back with legs bent at the knees. You can put your feet under a chair or have someone hold your feet down. Place hands behind head. Raise your head and shoulders about 30°, but keep your lower back on the floor or mat. Twist your torso at the same time to bring your right elbow over your left thigh. Then repeat, this time bringing your left elbow over your right thigh. Repeat five times on each side.

Exercise 2

Get someone to follow your instructions:

If you do exercises, describe how to do them in detail.

If you participate in sports, describe your favorite sport and briefly explain the rules, without mentioning the name of the sport.

See if people can guess which sport you have described.

Exercise 1

1. remind

She reminded them to fasten their seat belts.

2. warn

She warned them not to leave their seats.

Continue.

3. instruct	**8.** promise	**12.** urge
4. advise	**9.** tell	**13.** order
5. remind	**10.** help	**14.** urge
6. warn	**11.** tell	**15.** force
7. invite		

Exercise 2

Look at these sentences.
1. He said, "No, no…please don't shoot me."
2. She said, "Whatever you do, don't go to that dentist."
3. He said, "If I were you, I'd travel by train."
4. She said, "Would you like to come to a party on Saturday?"
5. She said, "Don't forget to go to the bank today."
6. The policeman said, "Turn off the engine, and get out of the car."
7. She said, "Don't worry. I'll definitely meet you at six o'clock."
8. The attendant said, "Would you mind moving your car?"
9. She said, "I'm too busy now. Call back later."

He begged her not to shoot him.

Continue, using these words:
warn/advise/invite/remind/order/promise/ask/tell.

Exercise 3

Practice with a partner (one of you is Student A, the other is Student B).

STUDENT A	STUDENT B
Ask B to meet you tonight.	Promise to meet A.
Advise B not to eat so much.	Tell A to mind his/her own business.
Ask B to write a letter from your dictation.	Ask A to speak more slowly.
Invite B to a party.	Refuse politely.
Order B to be quiet.	Tell A not to talk like that.
Remind B to repay the money you lent him/her.	Promise to pay tomorrow.
Order B to jump out of the window.	Tell A not to be so silly.
Warn B not to go over the speed limit.	Tell A to watch out for the police!

🎧 Listening 1

Rosa Sampson is a secretary at Standard Security Systems. Her boss, Peter Daniels, was away on business on Monday. She took several messages for him. Listen to the conversations and look at the messages.

It's Tuesday morning. Peter Daniels has just returned to the office. Look at the messages and listen to Rosa's report.

Peter: Good morning, Rosa. Could you come in for a minute, please?

Rosa: Good morning, Peter. Did you have a good trip?

Peter: Yes, thanks. It went very well.

Rosa: You had a few messages yesterday. Should I run through them?

Peter: Yes, go ahead.

Rosa: OK. Judy called. She said she wouldn't be in until Friday.

Peter: Oh? Why is that?

Rosa: She said she had the flu.

Peter: OK. What else?

Rosa: George came in looking for you. He said he wanted tomorrow off.

Peter: Did he say why?

Rosa: Yes. He told me his grandmother had died and he'd have to go to the funeral.

Peter: Oh, I'm sorry to hear that. I'd better talk to him later on.

Rosa: Then Joe Watkins called. He said he couldn't make the meeting this afternoon but would call you on Wednesday morning.

WHILE YOU WERE OUT

To: Peter Date: 3/23
From: Judy Time: 9:00 a.m.
Tel:
Message: *She has the flu. Won't be in till Friday.*

Urgent ☐ Returned call ☐ Call back ☐ Will call again ☐
Phoned ☑ Was in ☐ Wants to see you ☐
Operator: Rosa

WHILE YOU WERE OUT

To: Peter Date: 3/23
From: George Time: 11:40 a.m.
Tel:
Message: *Wants Wednesday off. Grandmother died. Will have to go to funeral.*

Urgent ☐ Returned call ☐ Call back ☑ Will call again ☐
Phoned ☐ Was in ☑ Wants to see you ☐
Operator: Rosa

WHILE YOU WERE OUT

To: Peter Date: 3/23
From: Joe Watkins Time: 3:20 p.m.
Tel:
Message: *Can't make meeting Tuesday p.m. He'll call you Wednesday a.m.*

Urgent ☐ Returned call ☐ Call back ☐ Will call again ☑
Phoned ☑ Was in ☐ Wants to see you ☐
Operator: Rosa

🎧 Listening 2

Imagine that you are the administrative assistant to Chris Matthews, who is out of the office for the day. Listen to the conversations and take messages.

To: *Chris Matthews* Date: Time: ☐ AM ☐ PM
WHILE YOU WERE OUT
M:
of
Phone: (   ) Area Code Number Extension
Telephoned ☐ Wants to see you ☐ Returned your call ☐
Urgent ☐ Will call again ☐ Called to see you ☐
Operator:

To: *Chris Matthews* Date: Time: ☐ AM ☐ PM
WHILE YOU WERE OUT
M:
of
Phone: (   ) Area Code Number Extension
Telephoned ☐ Wants to see you ☐ Returned your call ☐
Urgent ☐ Will call again ☐ Called to see you ☐
Operator:

To: *Chris Matthews* Date: Time: ☐ AM ☐ PM
WHILE YOU WERE OUT
M:
of
Phone: (   ) Area Code Number Extension
Telephoned ☐ Wants to see you ☐ Returned your call ☐
Urgent ☐ Will call again ☐ Called to see you ☐
Operator:

To: *Chris Matthews* Date: Time: ☐ AM ☐ PM
WHILE YOU WERE OUT
M:
of
Phone: (   ) Area Code Number Extension
Telephoned ☐ Wants to see you ☐ Returned your call ☐
Urgent ☐ Will call again ☐ Called to see you ☐
Operator:

Exercise 1

Report the messages to Chris Matthews. For example:

Wilson Auto Sales called. They said your new car wasn't ready yet.

Look at this:

am/is → was	"It's important." She said (that) it was important.
are → were	"They're going to be late." She said (that) they were going to be late.
have/has → had	"I've done the letters." She said (that) she had done the letters.
don't → didn't	"I don't know." She said (that) she didn't know.
want → wanted	"I want a day off." She said (that) she wanted a day off.
didn't do → hadn't done	"I didn't finish it." She said (that) she hadn't finished it.
saw → had seen	"I saw him." She said (that) she had seen him.
was/were → had been	"I wasn't there." She said (that) she hadn't been there.
will/won't → would/wouldn't	"I won't do it." She said (that) she wouldn't do it.
can/can't → could/couldn't	"I can't do it." She said (that) she couldn't do it.
may → might	"I may do it." She said (that) she might do it.

had done/would/could/ should/ought/might	No change.

When you are reporting, you may also need to change these words:

this → that
these → those
here → there
now → then

yesterday → the day before
tomorrow → the next day
this (week) → that (week)
last (month) → the (month) before
next (year) → the next (year)

Giving peace a chance

This is *One Hour* and I'm Barbara Waters. Tonight, an interview with Sandistan's Prime Minister Simon Prokowa, who earlier this week in Davos, Switzerland, signed an historic peace agreement between Sandistan and the new country of Deseret.

Waters: Good evening, Mr. Prime Minister.

Prokowa: Good evening.

Waters: Mr. Prime Minister, the world is simply amazed and delighted that your country signed this peace agreement. What was the immediate effect of this peace agreement?

Prokowa: The first thing was an immediate cease-fire.

Waters: Have both parties honored the cease-fire?

Prokowa: Oh, yes. So far.

Waters: What will happen next?

Prokowa: Well, now we have to begin talks to work out the details.

Waters: Are you going to relocate your citizens who live in the new country of Deseret?

Prokowa: That is one of the many things we have to work out. But will they want to be relocated? After all, they have built homes there. If they don't want to be relocated, can they continue to live there after our troops are no longer there to protect them?

Waters: Will the other people who live there be able to govern themselves?

Prokowa: That's a good question. I'm sure they want to govern themselves, but I'm not sure that that will be economically possible.

Waters: Do you think they can get help from other nations?

Prokowa: Absolutely. I'm sure Deseret's leaders would never have entered into these agreements without assurances of some economic aid.

Waters: Will you cooperate with the new government? After all, you once considered them rebels.

Prokowa: Well, we will have to move slowly, of course. But I'm sure that, with time, relations will become normal.

Waters: Are your people happy about the prospect of peace?

Prokowa: Those who believe that we will really have peace are happy. But some people are having trouble trusting our old enemies. They don't believe we are free from war and terrorism yet.

Waters: When do you think all the details will be settled?

Prokowa: It's hard to say. We are all willing to work very hard in the next few weeks. I would like to say that it will take one or two months, but I really don't know. It depends on how smoothly things go.

Waters: Where are you going to hold the first negotiations?

Prokowa: First we are going to Oslo, Norway. Then we are going to Paris. Maybe we won't have to go anywhere else after that.

Waters: Well, the whole world will be hoping for your success. Thank you for being with us here tonight, Mr. Prime Minister. Peace.

Look at this:

"What was the immediate effect of this peace agreement?"
She asked what the immediate effect of that peace agreement had been.

"The first thing was an immediate cease-fire."
He said that the first thing had been an immediate cease-fire.

"Have both parties honored the cease-fire?"
She asked if both parties had honored the cease-fire.

"Oh, yes. So far."
He said that both parties had so far.

Exercise 1

Look at the interview between Barbara Waters and Prime Minister Prokowa. Report all the questions and answers.

Exercise 2

Work with a partner. Role play an interview between a famous TV interviewer and a politician in the news.

Melissa sat alone by the empty swimming pool, watching the sun begin to set behind the palm trees into the ocean beyond. She sat as she had done so many times, thinking of that last fight two weeks before. She remembered how Don had at first denied being with Teresa, but then when she had forced him to admit it, how he had apologized and begged her for forgiveness. She frowned a little as she thought of her harsh words, and how Don, the only man she had ever really loved, had broken down and cried like a baby when she had refused to see him again. That was two weeks ago, and she had heard nothing from him since. She hadn't wanted to call him. She might want to admit that she had been unfair or to tell him how much she regretted calling him a liar. She might even say that she hadn't meant to hurt him. Then she would be a liar too. She had meant every word.

Suddenly, the sound of footsteps startled her. She turned and through the gloom she thought she could make out Don's familiar figure. Was it him? Could it possibly be? The approaching figure stepped into the last patch of sunlight, and the last rays of the setting sun illuminated his dark, curly hair. He stopped, unsure of himself. "Oh, Don," she said softly, trying to control her voice. "What are you doing here?"

"Melissa," he cried. "Don't send me away."

She sighed deeply as he ran to where she sat.

He took her hands tightly in his. "My darling," he whispered. "Can you ever forgive me?"

"I…," she started but checked herself. "I guess I'm partly to blame, but…"

He interrupted her. "That's all in the past. Let's not ever talk about it again—not ever…. Darling, promise me something?"

"What?" she asked cautiously.

"Here, this is for you. Please, please accept it, and wear it forever." He drew a small leather box from his pocket and leaned forward to give it to her. Suddenly, the box fell from his grasp. He bent to pick it up and at that moment his glasses slipped from his nose.

"Damn! Now where have they gone? I can't see a thing without them," he explained. Melissa leaned over the arm of her chair to help him. There was a crunch as his foot crushed the glasses. "Oh, no, now I've stepped on them!" he exclaimed. "Why can't I do anything right? Why do I always ruin everything?"

Her laughter pealed around the pool. "Oh, Don, you are incredible. Who could hate somebody like you? I might even love you. Come here."

Look at the pictures below. Make up stories about the weddings in each of the pictures. Would you get married on a ride or underwater? Why or why not?

"England and America are two countries divided by a common language."
GEORGE BERNARD SHAW

English is the mother tongue of approximately 450 million people today. But because of its importance as a language of business, science, and popular culture, it is spoken and/or understood by roughly one-third of the 5.5 billion people in the world.

Because of this, there are many varieties of English (American, British, Canadian, Australian, Jamaican, Indian, to name a few), as well as regional dialects. But despite the differences, all English speakers recognize that they are speaking the same basic language.

Or do they?

A NEW WORLD, A NEW LANGUAGE

When the English colonists arrived in North America, they found new people and languages. As they lived, fought, and traded with these people, many words, phrases, and usages were adopted into English. As early as 1720, people began to notice that a new, distinct English was forming.

Exercise 1

Below are a list of words "borrowed" from other languages. Match the words with their original language.

spaghetti	*French*
bagel	*Native American*
canyon	*Dutch*
rodeo	*Yiddish (Jewish)*
canoe	*French*
depot	*Spanish*
boss	*Italian*
tomato	*Native American*
levee	*Spanish*

GROWING APART

The industrial revolution in the nineteenth and early twentieth centuries increased the differences between American and British English. Because technology developed separately in both countries, different words were used to describe the same object. Some examples:

AMERICAN ENGLISH	BRITISH ENGLISH
theater	cinema
movie	film
expressway/parkway	motorway
truck	lorry
railroad	railway
landing gear	undercarriage
conductor	guard
streetcar	tram, trolley
subway	underground
TV	telly

Look at this:

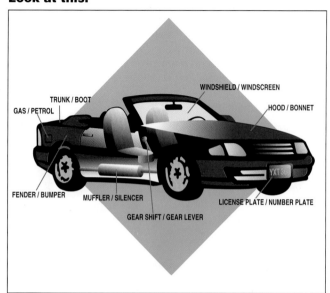

Labels: WINDSHIELD / WINDSCREEN · TRUNK / BOOT · GAS / PETROL · HOOD / BONNET · FENDER / BUMPER · MUFFLER / SILENCER · GEAR SHIFT / GEAR LEVER · LICENSE PLATE / NUMBER PLATE

COMING TOGETHER

As the twentieth century moved on, opportunities for communication between the two nations grew more frequent. World War II brought millions of American troops to Great Britain. Although there was some tension the end result was a closer relationship and language.

But the real driving force for coming together was popular culture. "Talking pictures" from the late 1920s, television, and rock music narrowed the gap by introducing idioms, words, and usages. This trend is accelerating today, with cheaper and quicker phone lines which allow data and video transmission throughout the world, and the spread of Hollywood movies and American TV worldwide.

Exercise 2

Below are pairs of words, each describing the same object or person. Do you know which are American and which are British?

garbage/rubbish	ground beef/minced beef
cabana/beach hut	VCR/video
pharmacist/chemist	yard/garden
cookie/biscuit	napkin/serviette
elevator/lift	aubergine/eggplant
drapes/curtains	trash basket/waste bin

NOTE: *All* of the American words would be understood by most British people.

Departures

Yoshiko Kyo has been studying English at a college in California. She'll finish the course at the end of this week. She's going back home to Tokyo on Saturday.

Streamline Taxis: Streamline Taxi.

Yoshiko: I'd like a cab to San Francisco International Airport for Saturday morning, please.

Taxis: OK.

Yoshiko: There'll be three of us. How much will it be?

Taxis: What's your address?

Yoshiko: I'm at 128 Cortland Avenue.

Taxis: We charge $45 for that trip.

Yoshiko: Forty-five dollars! Each?

Taxis: No. That's all together. What time do you want to leave?

Yoshiko: Check-in time is 12 noon, but I don't know how long it takes to get there.

Taxis: Well, we'd better pick you up at 11:00, just in case traffic is heavy. Let me have your name and address.

Yoshiko: Yes, OK. The first name is Yoshiko—that's Y-O-S-H-I-K-O—and the last name's Kyo—K-Y-O.

Taxis: Kyo. 128 Cortland Avenue. OK. Eleven o'clock Saturday morning. Thank you.

Mr. Berman: Come in.

Yoshiko: Hi, Mr. Berman. Do you have a minute? I just stopped in to say good-bye.

Mr. Berman: Oh…going back to Japan. When do you leave?

Yoshiko: Tomorrow. My flight is at two o'clock.

Mr. Berman: Well, have a good trip back. It's been nice having you here, Yoshiko.

Yoshiko: Thank you, Mr. Berman. Well…uh…I just wanted to thank you and all the other teachers.

Mr. Berman: We've all enjoyed having you as a student.

Yoshiko: I've really learned a lot. I hope to come back next year—on vacation.

Mr. Berman: Send us a postcard and let us know how you're doing, and come see us if you do get back.

Yoshiko: I'll do that.

Mr. Berman: Oh. There's the bell. Bye, Yoshiko. Have a good trip.

Yoshiko: Bye, Mr. Berman, and thanks again for everything.

Yoshiko: Carlos! I'm glad I didn't miss you.

Carlos: Hi, Yoshiko. When are you leaving?

Yoshiko: Tomorrow around eleven o'clock. I guess I won't see you again, so good-bye. It's been great knowing you.

Carlos: That sounds so final. Let's keep in touch, OK?

Yoshiko: Oh, sure. You have my address, don't you?

Carlos: Yeah, and remember, if you're ever in Caracas, look me up. I'd love to see you again.

Yoshiko: Oh, I will. You can count on that. And you do the same if you're ever in Tokyo.

Carlos: Sure. Well…good-bye.

Yoshiko: Bye, Carlos. Take care.

Mrs. Simmons: Yoshiko! The taxi's here. Are you ready? Do you have everything?

Yoshiko: Yes, thank you, Mrs. Simmons. And…thank you again.

Mrs. Simmons: Thank you, Yoshiko, for the pretty plant. Now don't forget to write as soon as you get home—just to let us know that you got there safe and sound.

Yoshiko: OK. Or maybe I'll call when the long-distance rates are low. The time difference is a mess, but I'll make sure I don't call in the middle of the night.

Mrs. Simmons: You're so sweet, Yoshiko. Good-bye now. You'd better not keep the taxi waiting. Travel safely. Bye.

Yoshiko: Bye. Take care. Say good-bye to Mr. Simmons for me…bye!

Exercise 1

Discuss: How are the customs for saying good-bye in American English the same as or different from your language and culture? Are there any differences for males and females in your language?

Exercise 2

Role play in pairs. Take turns ordering a taxi, saying good-bye to a teacher, saying good-bye to a classmate, and saying good-bye to a sponsor.

Irregular verbs

Infinitive form	Past tense	Past participle	Infinitive form	Past tense	Past participle
be	was/were	been	let	let	let
become	became	become	lose	lost	lost
begin	began	begun	make	made	made
break	broke	broken	mean	meant	meant
bring	brought	brought	meet	met	met
build	built	built	pay	paid	paid
buy	bought	bought	put	put	put
catch	caught	caught	read	read	read
choose	chose	chosen	ride	rode	ridden
come	came	come	ring	rang	rung
cost	cost	cost	run	ran	run
cut	cut	cut	say	said	said
do	did	done	see	saw	seen
drink	drank	drunk	sell	sold	sold
drive	drove	driven	send	sent	sent
eat	ate	eaten	shine	shone	shone
fall	fell	fallen	show	showed	shown
feel	felt	felt	shut	shut	shut
fight	fought	fought	sing	sang	sung
find	found	found	sit	sat	sat
fly	flew	flown	sleep	slept	slept
forget	forgot	forgotten	speak	spoke	spoken
freeze	froze	frozen	spend	spent	spent
get	got	gotten	stand	stood	stood
give	gave	given	steal	stole	stolen
go	went	gone	swim	swam	swum
grow	grew	grown	take	took	taken
have	had	had	teach	taught	taught
hear	heard	heard	tear	tore	torn
hide	hid	hidden	tell	told	told
hit	hit	hit	think	thought	thought
hurt	hurt	hurt	throw	threw	thrown
keep	kept	kept	wake	woke	woken
know	knew	known	wear	wore	worn
leave	left	left	win	won	won
lend	lent	lent	write	wrote	written

Listening appendix

Unit 1

1.
Air Streamline flight 604 departing at 2:45 for JFK Airport in New York City is now boarding at Gate 3. Passengers with tickets on Air Streamline flight 604 at 2:45 to New York please proceed to Gate 3.

2.
This is the last call for Global Airlines flight 373 departing at 2:30 for Houston. Passengers on Global flight 373 at 2:30 to Houston should board now at Gate 1.

3.
Crossland Airlines announces that flight 127 to Houston and El Paso is now scheduled to depart at 3:00 from Gate 7. Passengers on Crossland 127 are advised that their flight will depart from Gate 7 at 3:00.

4.
Global Airlines announces that flight 881 to New York City's La Guardia Airport at 2:55 will depart from Gate 2 and will start boarding in ten minutes. At this time, will passengers with small children and those who need special help in boarding, please go to Gate 2 for Global flight 881 to New York La Guardia at 2:55?

5.
Air Streamline flight 403 to Atlanta, with connections to Miami and other points south, will depart on schedule at 3:05 from Gate 4. We repeat: Air Streamline 403 will depart as scheduled at 3:05 for Atlanta. Passengers should make their seat selection at Gate 4 prior to boarding, which will begin in five minutes.

Unit 7

Report 2

Cindy Wong: I'm standing in front of the only house still occupied on the 800 block of Sheridan Street. We have managed to set up an interview with Mrs. Florence Hamilton, the occupant of the house. She has decided to speak to us, but she has demanded to see me alone except for a camera crew of two.

Mrs. Hamilton, our viewers would like to hear your side of the story.

Hamilton: There's not much to say. They want me to move. I was born here, and I intend to die here. It's as simple as that…. Down Caesar! Sit! Cleo! Sit!

Cindy: But the Housing Authority really needs to have this land, and they have arranged to relocate you.

Hamilton: I know. But I can't take all my dogs, just one. I love them all, and I need to have company. They're all I have. Come back, Calpurnia! Sit! Sit!

Cindy: How long can you hold out here?

Hamilton: Oh, I have plenty of food. People bring me dog food. The city has threatened to cut off my water and lights, but I'll be all right.

Cindy: Thank you, Mrs. Hamilton.

Hamilton: You can tell the city for me that I want a house where I can keep my dogs, not a [bleep] apartment for [bleep] senior citizens!

Cindy: Uh, yes…uh, this has been Cindy Wong talking to Mrs. Florence Hamilton, who is fighting to keep her home and pets, for Channel 7 Newsdesk. Back to you in the studio, Katy.

Unit 9

Dr. Sisters: Jonathan! I'm so glad you could come.

Jonathan: Hello, Dr. Sisters. Well, I'll be honest. Barbara had to force me to come, really.

Dr. Sisters: Does it embarrass you to talk about your problems?

Jonathan: Yes, it does. But I guess we need to talk to somebody.

Dr. Sisters: Barbara feels that you…well, that you resent her job.

Jonathan: I don't know. I'd like her to stay home, but she's very smart. So really, I encouraged her to go back to work. With the kids in school, she needs something to do. And I suppose we need the money.

Dr. Sisters: How do you share the housework?

Jonathan: I try to help. I always help her with the dishes, and I help Gary and Debbie to do their homework while she makes dinner. But she doesn't think that's enough. What do you think?

Dr. Sisters: I'm not here to give an opinion, Jonathan.

Jonathan: I think we're both too tired, that's all. In the evenings we're both too tired to talk. And Barbara…she never allows me to suggest anything about the house or about the kids. We always have the same arguments. She has her own opinions and that's it. Last night we had another fight. She's forbidden the kids to ride their bikes to school.

Dr. Sisters: Why?

Jonathan: She thinks they're too young to ride in traffic. But then she always complains about picking them up at her sister's. I mean…they can't be tied to their mother's apron strings all their lives, can they?

Unit 11 (part 1)

Listening 1

P Would you turn down the radio, please?
I Would you turn down the radio, please?
P Would you turn down the radio, please?

I Open the door, please.
P Open the door, please.
P Open the door, please.

P Could you make a copy of this?
I Could you make a copy of this?
I Could you make a copy of this?

I Can I use your stapler?
P Can I use your stapler?
I Can I use your stapler?

P Would you please take our picture?
I Would you please take our picture?
I Would you please take our picture?

I Can I get change for a dollar?
I Can I get change for a dollar?
P Can I get change for a dollar?

Listening 2

1.
M: Hurry up. We're going to be late. The train leaves in half an hour.
F: Really? I thought we had plenty of time.
M: [Students predict tone of speaker. Five-second pause.] Could you walk a little faster, please? (Impolite)

2.
M: Hello. I'd like to deposit this check.
F: Certainly. Oh, you forgot to endorse it.
M: [Students predict tone of speaker. Five-second pause.] Can I use that pen? (Polite)

3.
M1: Kevin!
M2: Oh, hi, Dad. What's up?
M1: [Students predict tone of speaker. Five-second pause.] Would you mind turning off the TV? (Impolite)

Unit 13

Listening 1

1.
This is the last call for flight 932 to Syracuse, now boarding at Gate 14. Scheduled departure time is 3:25 PM.

2.
Flight 217 with nonstop service to Caracas is boarding at Gate 34. The flight is ten minutes behind schedule and will depart at 3:40 PM.

3.
Flight 558, with service to Hartford, Connecticut, and Springfield, Massachusetts, is now ready for boarding at Gate 26. The flight will depart on schedule at 3:45 PM.

4.
Air USA flight 563 to Detroit is now preboarding. Passengers with small children or who require special help in boarding should go now to Gate 12. The flight will leave as scheduled at 4:30.

5.
Will Air USA passenger Rita Chambers holding a ticket on flight 67, scheduled to depart for San Francisco at 4:30, please go to Gate 32 for a new seat assignment prior to boarding? Ms. Rita Chambers, please report to Gate 32.

6.
Passengers for Los Angeles, may I please have your attention. Air USA's nonstop service to Los Angeles, flight 811, scheduled to depart at 4:30, has been delayed due to late arrival from London. Flight 811 will now depart at 4:50 from Gate 30. Boarding will begin in 15 minutes.

Listening 2

1.
Good afternoon, ladies and gentlemen. This is your captain, Tom Brown. We'd like to welcome you aboard flight 811 and to apologize for the delay. We had some bumpy weather over the Atlantic, and arrived late from London. Now we are experiencing another slight delay as we wait for clearance from Air Traffic Control. We don't expect it will be more than five minutes, and we hope to arrive in Los Angeles at about 7:30 local time.

2.
This is the captain again. I just wanted to apologize again for the delays and to let you know that we are almost back on schedule. Our Boeing 767 is cruising at an altitude of about 30,000 feet at an airspeed of, oh, around 560 miles per hour. We are above the state of Maryland and that's Washington, DC, over to the left of the plane. The temperature in Los Angeles is 79° Fahrenheit (that's 26° Centigrade), and it's sunny and clear—really unusual for Los Angeles. We ask that while you are in your seats you keep your seat belts fastened, just in case we hit some unexpected turbulence.

3.
Ladies and gentlemen, we are beginning our approach now to Los Angeles International Airport. Please make sure your seat belt is securely fastened, and return your seat and tray to their original upright positions.

4.
We hope you have had a pleasant and enjoyable flight, and we'd like to thank you for flying Air USA today. Please remain in your seat until the plane has come to a complete and final stop at the gate. If you have any questions about connecting flights, please see the Air USA agents who will meet our flight. On behalf of Captain Tom Brown and the rest of the crew, thanks again for flying Air USA!

Unit 14

Mindy: MacGizmos. This is Mindy speaking. How can I help you?
Caller: Hi. I'd like to order some software, please.
Mindy: Do you have a catalog number?
Caller: Yes, I do. It's GKX 371 243.

Mindy: Please hold…that's the "Death Star Defender" game on CD-ROM for Macintosh?

Caller: That's right.

Mindy: What city?

Caller: I'm calling from London, in Britain.

Mindy: May I have your name and address?

Caller: Yes. It's Simon Alton, that's A-L-T-O-N, 42 Gladstone Terrace, London W6 8BN, England.

Mindy: Simon Alton, 42 Gladstone Terrace, London, W6 8BN, England? And how do you want that sent, Simon? Surface, air, or courier?

Caller: Courier.

Mindy: That will be a total of $89.30, including delivery.

Caller: Fine.

Mindy: And how are you paying?

Caller: MasterCard®.

Mindy: May I have your number?

Caller: 5055 6631 8901 4247.

Mindy: 5055 6631 8901 4247. And the expiration date on the card?

Caller: September next year.

Mindy: And what is the name actually printed on the card?

Caller: Simon W. Alton.

Mindy: That's great, Simon. Your CD-ROM will be there in a few days. Thank you for calling MacGizmos.

Unit 15

Lynn: Excuse me. How much do you want for this bowl?

Stand owner: Let's see. Hmm…. That's an outstanding piece of Depression glass—in perfect shape. It's worth 150 bucks.

Lynn: A hundred and fifty dollars! Oh, I couldn't possibly pay that much. It's a shame. It really is nice.

Owner: Hold on, lady. I said it was worth 150 bucks. I'm only asking $115.

Lynn: A hundred and fifteen dollars?

Owner: Yeah, it's a real bargain.

Lynn: Oh, I'm sure it is. But I can't afford that.

Owner: Well, look. Tell you what I'll do. I'll make it an even $100. I can't go any lower than that.

Lynn: I'll give you $65.

Owner: Sixty-five! Come on, lady. You've got to be kidding. I paid more than that for it myself. Take it for $90. It's worth every penny.

Lynn: Well, maybe I could give you $75.

Owner: Eighty-five. That's my final price.

Lynn: Eighty.

Owner: Make it $83.

Lynn: OK. Eighty-three.

Owner: Let me wrap it up for you. There you are, lady—a real bargain.

Lynn: Yeah, thanks a lot.

Unit 19

In the cabin, the flight attendants and the doctor were busy attending to the sick. Several people were unconscious. The plane circled for over half an hour. The passengers had begun to realize that something was wrong. "What's going on? Why don't we land?" shouted one man. "We've got to get my wife to the hospital!" A woman began sobbing quietly. At last the plane started its descent. Suddenly there was a bump that shook the plane. "We're all going to die!" screamed a man. Even the flight attendants looked worried. "It's all right!" someone said. "The pilot just lowered the landing gear, that's all." As the plane approached the runway they could see fire trucks and ambulances speeding along the runway with their lights flashing. There was a tremendous thump as the wheels hit the tarmac, bounced twice, raced along the runway, and screeched to a halt. The first airport truck was there in seconds. "That was nearly a perfect landing. Good job!" shouted the air-traffic controller. "Thanks," said the man. "Any chance of a job?"

Unit 24

I was out by the pond, fishing in my usual spot. When I heard the shots, I hurried through the trees toward the house. I saw Benson running across the lawn toward the study. When I got there, everybody was in the room. Poor old Charlie was dead. I know a dead man when I see one. After all, I was in the army during the war.

Unit 40

When you're visiting northern California, be sure to come to Dr. Bronner's Hot Springs Spa in beautiful, relaxing Calistoga for a fabulous health-break. For just $69, you'll get a complete health treatment: mud bath, mineral bath, sauna, steam wrap, and massage. We guarantee that you'll come out feeling refreshed, rejuvenated, and just plain terrific—all for only $69!

You can stay at Dr. Bronner's overnight for just $94. All the rooms are spacious and quiet, with large private baths. They all have color TVs, mini-refrigerators, and microwaves. Your comfort is our business!

We're conveniently located on Lincoln Avenue, just one block from the Calistoga Bookstore. For reservations, call 1-707-555-2478.

Unit 43

Kaye Wilson: I went to a big high school in the Midwest. We lived in a well-to-do suburb, so the school was pretty good academically. I wish my parents had let me take more science and math courses. No, I wish I had insisted on taking what I wanted to. For college they sent me East to a fancy girls school. For them, girls went to college only to meet the "right boy" and, as a second thought, to "have something to fall back on" in case your husband died, and you had to go to work. I thought they were right and I was wrong, so I majored in literature. I never met the right boy.

Instead of falling back on teaching literature, I'm in advertising. In fact, I'm the vice president of my agency. It's OK, but if I had taken the subjects I wanted, I would be an engineer or…an astronaut. I wish my teachers had given me better advice. I'm really sorry my parents didn't let me do what I wanted.

Unit 44

1.

Adam: Hi there!

Tony: Hi. Aren't you that guy from TV?

Adam: That's right.

Tony: Yeah! You're Alan Vasquez.

Adam: Uh, that's *Adam* Vasquez…. Are you having a good time tonight?

Tony: Yeah!

Adam: What's your name?

Tony: Uh…this is Tony King talking to you from Times Square! Hi, Mom! Hi, Dad!

Adam: Where are you from, Tony?

Tony: Boston. I'm a student here in New York.

Adam: A student, huh? Well, you have one wish, Tony. What are you going to wish for?

Tony: Good grades. That's my wish for next year. Good grades.

Adam: Thanks, Tony.

2.

Adam: Pardon me, ma'am. Can I ask you a few questions?

Susan: Sure. Go right ahead.

Adam: You're on network TV. Tell me about yourself.

Susan: Well, my name's Susan Lee, and I live here in New York. I'm a teacher. I teach second grade.

Adam: Great. If you had one wish for next year, what would it be?

Susan: Wow! Let me think. Something for the children…I just wish that all people could live together in peace and harmony. You know, no more racial prejudice and wars….

Adam: That's great. Really great, Susan.

3.

Adam: Excuse me…

Peter: Me?

Adam: Yes, you sir. Can I ask you some questions?

Peter: OK.

Adam: What's your name?

Peter: My name is Peter. Peter Kowalski.

Adam: Do you live here in New York?

Peter: Yes, I do. I've been here for three years. I like it very much.

Adam: Where do you come from?

Peter: I am from Poland. I am working here as a cab driver.

Adam: Are you enjoying New Year's Eve?

Peter: Yes. It is very good.

Adam: If you could make one wish—just one wish—what would you wish for?

Peter: So many things. I wish I could travel back home this year and see my grandparents.

Adam: I hope your wish comes true, Peter.

Peter: Thank you. But first I have to save my money!

4.

Diane: Hi. Am I on TV?

Adam: Hi. Yes, you are.

Diane: What show is it?

Adam: It's the *Adam Vasquez Show*. Do you watch it?

Diane: Nah. I always watch David Letterman.

Adam: I see. Do you want to give anyone a message?

Diane: Wow! I just want to say hi to everyone at Bernard's Burger Bar in Washington, DC. And a happy new year!

Adam: OK. While you're here, can I ask you some questions?

Diane: Sure.

Adam: So, you're from Washington?

Diane: That's right. I'm a waitress at Bernard's Burger Bar. And my name's Diane…Diane Kelly.

Adam: OK, Diane. We're going to let you make one wish. What would you wish for?

Diane: This is really wild! Uh, I'd wish for an end to all the street crime. You know, the streets aren't safe anymore.

Adam: Thank you. OK…it's nearly ten seconds to midnight, and we're counting down…10!

Crowd: -9-8-7-6-5-4-3-2-Happy New Year!!!

Unit 48

Listening 1

Caroline Newton, who was kidnapped last Monday, has been found safe and sound. The 14-year-old, whose parents are well-known and wealthy doctors, was found by police in a house in Bayside, only 20 miles from her home. The alleged kidnappers, who were arrested and charged by police last night, rented the house under the name "Mr. and Mrs. Harry Gilmore." Neighbors, who were suspicious of the new renters, called police. The suspects, whose real names are Jill and Andrew Roland, confessed to the crime. They had sent a note to the girl's parents demanding $1,000,000.

Listening 2

The so-called wonder drug Kural, which some doctors have been recommending as a painkiller, has been banned by the federal Food and Drug Administration. After extensive clinical tests, which were first demanded by Ralph Raider, the drug has been found to produce alarming side effects in laboratory mice. The ban stated that while Kural is certainly an effective painkiller, the drug "speeds up the aging process, which leads to premature hair loss, stiffening of the joints, and loss of memory."

Unit 52

Donna

Well, she's really talkative and funny. She's about—well, in her late teens. She's pretty tall with a really good figure. She has a kind of oval-shaped face, and a turned-up nose—very pretty in a way. She has long, wavy black hair and…uh…blue eyes with very long eyelashes. Her complexion is—well, she's olive-skinned. Her lips are very full, and she has dimples—the cutest little dimples in her cheeks. Oh, and she always wears jeans.

Tony

He's a really big guy, you know, well-built with very broad shoulders. Not fat at all, but solid. He's in his early thirties. He's dark-skinned, and he has a long face with thin lips. Oh, and a scar on his chin. He has dark curly hair, almost black, and wears it short but with long sideburns and a mustache. His eyes…I haven't really noticed the color—he wears glasses—brown, I guess. He has thick eyebrows and kind of a long, straight nose. He's pretty reserved and quiet, sometimes even moody.

Janet

She's very sophisticated. Well-dressed, one of those expensive haircuts, you know. I'd say she was in her late thirties or early forties, but she looks younger. She's about average height and very slim. Her hair's very blond—dyed, I think, but I'm not sure. It's always very neat, not long. She has light gray eyes with thin eyebrows. Her face is always suntanned and very well made up. It's an attractive face—not really beautiful, but attractive—handsome, if you know what I mean. High cheekbones, small chin—oh, and there's a beauty mark on her left cheek. She's a very confident and reliable sort of person, very sociable and always very, very polite.

Bob

Bob's a terrific person. He's elderly but not really old—cheerful and friendly and funny. He's probably in his early seventies. He has white hair, receding a little, and a small white beard. He's of medium build, a little bit overweight maybe. He has nice, big, brown eyes, and he always seems to be smiling—lots of wrinkles around the eyes, but they're smile lines, not frown lines. He has a very high, lined forehead that makes him look very intelligent—which he is, of course.

Unit 59

Listening 1

Fred: Where's a map?

Alice: There's one over here. They said we have to meet them at Farragut North. Can you find it?

Fred: Yes, here it is. I guess we take the Blue Line to L'Enfant Plaza, then change to the Yellow Line and go to Gallery Place. Then we go two stops to Farragut North on the Red Line.

Alice: I'm not sure that's the quickest way. We could take the Blue Line all the way to Metro Center and get the Red Line there. Then it's only one stop.

Fred: We might as well do it your way. It's only one change. My way has two changes.

Listening 2

Fred: Where are we going now?

Alice: The Washington Monument. Here's the map I picked up.

Fred: OK. Let's see. Here we are—at Union Station. I think the best way to go is to take the Red Line three stops to Metro Center.

Alice: Right. And then we switch to either the Blue Line or the Orange Line—it doesn't seem to matter. So we take the Blue or the Orange Line south to the second stop.

Fred: Great. It shouldn't take long.

Unit 65

Peter: And now it's time for the "Star Gaze Minute" with your host, Cindy Barrett!

Cindy: Hi, everyone. I'm Cindy Barrett and have I got news for you…

This exclusive just in: The 37-year-old Duchess of Lichtenburg is planning a "secret wedding" in Monte Carlo in June. But you'll never guess who she's marrying—her limo driver! I guess the multimillionaire got tired of the single life, or it got tired of her…

Hugely successful thriller writer Michael Brighton is getting a divorce from his wife of 21 years. She must not fit in with his new Beverly Hills mansion, his sports cars, or his late-night lifestyle…

Beautiful and talented Julia Robbins will star as an American tourist on vacation in Europe. The 18-year-old actress will be getting a cool ten million dollars for her role. This will certainly help pay her legal fees from her messy court case against her former employer, World Studios.

Is handsome Oscar-winning Keith Southern, who just broke off his engagement to supermodel Kate Roth, dating someone new? Friends of the 30-year-old Keith say no, but we've all seen the pictures of his romantic, candle-lit dinner with yet another super-beautiful supermodel, Corrine Collins. I'm sure we'll hear more about this couple…

Talented wealthy singer Niles Lovitt, who just got a divorce from his first wife of 15 years, is going to be an actor! Sources say that the country-and-western superstar will play the lead role in the movie *Country Living*.

And finally, sexy 35-year-old Senator from Nebraska Jenny Doright has been dancing the night away at all the hottest Washington and New York nightspots—while her husband stays home with the twins! The mother of two, famous as the first woman to walk in space (in a stylish jumpsuit!), is the youngest female Senator in history.

That's all for now. More star news tomorrow. Back to you, Peter.

Unit 72

Real Estate Agent: I'm afraid it hasn't been kept up very well. The man who lived here was in his eighties when he died a few months ago. His daughter doesn't want the place, so she's selling it.

Robin: It looks as though it needs a lot of work done on it.

Agent: True, but the price is very reasonable. It could be a great do-it-yourself project.

Gene: Hmm. I'm not that good with my hands. We'd have to get most of the work done for us…

Robin: Oh, I don't know. Let's look at the inside.

Agent: Oh, sure. Let's go in through the kitchen door.

Robin: *Whew!* Look at that sink. It must have been there since the house was built.

Gene: The kitchen's big, though, and has plenty of light. We always wanted an eat-in kitchen. We'd have to have all new cabinets and major appliances—new stove, refrigerator, dishwasher…

Robin: Well, we'd have to start with having new plumbing installed. And we'd have to do something about this floor. I guess we could put down new tiles ourselves.

Gene: Yeah, you're right. Is that the only electrical outlet there?

Agent: I'm afraid it is.

Gene: It looks pretty old. I'm sure the whole place would need rewiring. We'd certainly have to have that done even before the plumbing. We would need a lot more outlets too.

Agent: Would you like to see the rest of the house? The dining room and living room are through here.

Robin: Oh, wow! These walls! I guess we'd have to cover all the walls with plasterboard.

Gene: That's easier said than done. We'd have to get somebody to put up the plasterboard; then we could do the painting. And, of course, the ceilings need painting, but we could do that too. What's the upstairs like?

Agent: More of the same. As you say, all the walls and ceilings need work, but look at these floors. They're

beautiful, aren't they? Now, as you know, there's no bathroom.

Robin: Yes, I noticed the bathtub in the kitchen. What about the toilet?

Agent: In the little outhouse in back. Anyway, I was about to say that you could have the small bedroom upstairs converted into a bathroom.

Gene: More plumbing costs, but of course we'd have to have it done. We couldn't live without indoor plumbing.

Robin: Absolutely. Is there anything else that has to be done?

Agent: Well, you'd have to get the roof repaired pretty soon.

Robin: The sooner the better if you ask me. It looks like water has been coming in over there.

Gene: And we'd have to have a new oil burner put in, I guess. Plus, we'd have to have the windows weatherproofed to keep the heat in during the winter. Hmm…I bet it'll cost a fortune to heat this place.

Agent: Well, of course, you'd want to insulate before you have the plasterboard put on.

Gene: Yeah, I guess we could put in the insulation. So, when it comes down to it the only things we can do are put down the new tiles, put in the insulation, and paint the place.

Robin: Right, and I wonder how good a job we'd do even with that. Well, thanks for showing us around, but I think we'd be better off knocking it down and starting all over again.

Unit 75

Listening 1

9:00

Rosa: Good morning. Peter Daniels' office.

Judy: Hi, Rosa. It's Judy. Can you give Peter a message, please? I won't be in until Friday. I have the flu. I saw the doctor this morning.

Rosa: OK, Judy. I'll give him the message. I hope you feel better soon.

11:40

George: Hi, Rosa.

Rosa: Hi, George. What can I do for you?

George: Peter isn't there, is he?

Rosa: No, he won't be in until tomorrow.

George: Well, it's just that I need Wednesday off. You see, my grandmother died yesterday and I'll have to go to the funeral.

Rosa: Oh, I'm sorry. How old was she?

George: Ninety-two.

3:20

Rosa: Peter Daniels' office. May I help you?

Joe: May I speak to Mr. Daniels, please?

Rosa: I'm sorry. He's out of the office today. He'll be back tomorrow. May I take a message?

Joe: This is Joe Watkins calling. Please tell Peter that I can't make the meeting tomorrow afternoon. Something important's come up. I'll call him Wednesday morning.

Listening 2

9:15

Administrative Assistant: Chris Matthews' office.

Sales Associate: I'd like to speak to Chris Matthews, please.

Assistant: I'm sorry. She isn't in today. Would you like to leave a message?

Associate: Sure. I'm calling from Wilson Auto Sales. It's about her new car. It isn't ready yet. There was a mix-up at the factory.

10:30

Assistant: Good morning, Chris Matthews' office.

John: Good morning. This is John North from Jannick International. May I speak to Ms. Matthews, please?

Assistant: Ms. Matthews is out of the office today. Would you like to leave a message?

John: Just tell her I called. I'll be out of my office tomorrow, but I'll try to reach her from where I'll be.

Assistant: OK, Mr. North. And what company did you say you were from?

John: Jannick International. That's J-A-N-N-I-C-K International.

1:10

Assistant: Good afternoon, Chris Matthews' office.

Anne: Good afternoon. This is Anne Mori from Western Video Systems. Chris is at the trade show in Chicago, isn't she?

Assistant: Yes, that's right. She should be here tomorrow.

Anne: Well, can you give her this message first thing in the morning? I'm afraid we have to cancel our last order. The customers have changed their minds again.

Assistant: OK. And could you spell your name for me, please?

Anne: Sure. That's Anne, A-N-N-E, Mori, M-O-R-I.

Assistant: Thanks. I'll give Chris the message.

3:35

Assistant: Chris Matthews' office.

Susan: Hello. Is Ms. Matthews in?

Assistant: No, she'll be here tomorrow morning. May I take a message?

Susan: My name is Susan Ellis, E-L-L-I-S. Would you have her call me as soon as she gets in? It's urgent.

Unit 78

Simon and Rachel were married recently at Walt Disney World in Florida. Their wedding was "A Disney Fairy Tale Wedding."

Rachel: When Simon and I met three years ago, I remember telling all my friends that he was my Prince Charming. Later, when we had gotten to know each other really well, I told him about it, so he started calling me *Cinderella.* Right after we decided to get married, we heard that we could get married at Disney World—well, not in the park itself, but at the hotels that are part of Disney World. We couldn't resist!

Simon: Rachel looked beautiful. She was wearing a long, white satin gown and she rode to the reception in a glass carriage drawn by six magnificent white horses. I was waiting for her outside the hotel, along with 100 guests.

Rachel: The ceremony was lovely. We had decided to write our own vows. But apart from that, we had the usual traditional service. We brought along our own minister from Cincinnati, and my maid of honor was my sister. Simon's best man was his best friend, and the ushers and bridesmaids were friends and cousins. All the men wore tuxedos and all the women wore long gowns. I walked down the aisle to the traditional "Here Comes the Bride." But after the ceremony, Simon and I walked out to the theme of "Beauty and the Beast."

Simon: The reception was amazing. It all took place in front of a 60-foot-tall replica of Cinderella's castle, complete with twinkling lights. Actors playing the roles of the Fairy Godmother and Cinderella's stepsisters mingled with the guests. Between eating and dancing—you know, the normal things that people do at weddings—there were three stage shows. For the finale, the cast performed "When You Wish Upon a Star" and fireworks erupted from the roof.

Rachel: The food was wonderful, by the way, and fit into the whole Cinderella theme. For dessert, each guest got a chocolate slipper filled with mousse. When it was time for us to leave, we got back into the glass carriage and rode away. It was a beautiful day, a real fairy tale come true. And now we get to live happily ever after.

Grammar summaries

Unit 1

Greetings

Formal
A: *Good morning/afternoon/evening.*
B: *Good morning/afternoon/evening.*
Formal (on being introduced)
A: *How do you do?*
B: *How do you do?*
Polite, friendly
A: *Hello. How are you?*
B: *Very well, thanks, and you?*
A: *I'm fine, thanks.*
Familiar, casual
A: *Hi!*
B: *Hi!*
A: *How are things?/How are you doing?/How are you getting along?*
B: *All right./OK./Not bad.*

Introductions

I'd like you to meet…/May I introduce…?/Hello, I'm…

Polite inquiries and responses

A: *How's work/the family? / How are (Larry and the kids)?*
B: *All right./OK./Fine.*
A: *Did you have a good trip?*

Thanking

A: *Thanks./Thank you./Thank you for coming to meet me.*
B: *It's a pleasure./That's all right./Not at all.*

Apologies

Sorry./I'm so sorry.
I'm afraid not.

Unit 2

Future continuous

I/You	'll		at 6.
He/She/It	will	be doing that	from 6 until 7.
We/They	won't		during the program.
	will not		for 10 minutes.

Future arrangements

The flight <u>leaves</u> at 8:30.
<u>I'm meeting</u> him tomorrow.
<u>We'll begin</u> at about 6:30.

Unit 3

Personal information

Name: *What's your name? I'm/My name's (William Paine).*
Date & place of birth: *When/Where were you born? I was born (on July 2) in (Providence, Rhode Island).*
Nationality: *Where are you from?/Where do you come from? I'm (American)./I am from (the United States/Rhode Island/Providence).*
Marital status: *Are you married? Yes, I am./No, I'm not. I'm single.*
Address: *What's your address?/Where do you live? I live at/My address is (77 Sunshine Boulevard).*
Education: *Where did you go to school/college? I went to (Whitney High School/Yale University).*
Occupation: *What do you do?/What's your job? I'm (an actor).*

Unit 4

Future perfect

| How | far | will | he | have | driven? |
| | many miles | | they | | gone? |

| He | 'll | have | driven | 500 miles. |
| They | will | | gone | very far. |

Comparison of adjectives

big/bigger/biggest/… as big as …
economical/more economical/most economical

Unit 5

Verb + -*ing* form

I	enjoy	doing this.
	love	
	like	
	don't like	
	dislike	
	can't stand	
	hate	
	don't mind	

I'm	afraid of	doing that.
	terrified of	
	frightened of	
	scared of	
	tired of	
	bored (with)	
	fed up with	
	interested in	

I	began	doing this.
	started	
	stopped	
	gave up	

Unit 6

Business letters

Salutations

When writing to…	Example
Someone with whom you are on a first-name basis, you can use the person's first name.	Mr. Robert Brown National Home Corp. 473 N. 6 Street Fairfield, IA 52556 *Dear Robert:*
A man you don't know, use the title *Mr.*	Mr. Victor Semple Western Insurance Co. 32 Meadowlands Parkway Secaucus, NJ 07094 *Dear Mr. Semple:*
A woman you don't know, use the title *Ms.*[1]	Ms. Sherry Greenspan Greenspan and Diamond 1497 Alameda Avenue Los Angeles, CA 90212 *Dear Ms. Greenspan:*
A person you don't know, whose gender is not clear from the name, use the person's full name.	Terry Murphy 659 Madison Avenue New York, NY 10018 *Dear Terry Murphy:*

When writing to an organization and you don't know the name or title of the recipient…[2]	Example
In formal correspondence, use a general salutation.[3]	*Dear Sir or Madam:* or *Dear Madam or Sir:*
In informal or routine correspondence, you can use the name of the organization: or the name of the department:	*Dear PhotoMart:* *Dear Parts Manager:*

Complimentary closings

Formal:	*Sincerely yours,*
Less Formal:	*Sincerely,*
Informal:	*Regards,*

Notes
1. If the woman has expressed a preference for *Mrs.* or *Miss,* honor her preference.
2. If you know the recipient's name but use an *Attention* line, you should use *Dear Sir or Madam,* since technically you are writing to the organization, not the individual. For this reason, it's better to avoid the *Attention* line.

Western Insurance Co.
32 Meadowlands Parkway
Secaucus, NJ 07094

Attention: Mr. Victor Semple

Dear Sir or Madam:

3. If possible, find out the name and title of the recipient.

Unit 7

Verb + infinitive

hope	to (do)
refuse	
plan	
offer	
agree	
want	
would like	
intend	
expect	
promise	
manage	
decide	
demand	
need	
arrange	
threaten	
had	
have	
going	

Unit 8

Adjective + infinitive

I	'm am was	delighted to (get)… sorry to (hear)… upset to (hear)…
He She	is was	lucky to (have)… sad to (learn)…
We You They	are were	ready to (help)… willing to (listen)… surprised to (find out)… anxious to (hear)…

It	is was will be has been	great to (see)… nice to (know)… wonderful to (hear)… interesting to (look at)… hard to (be)… difficult to (do)…

Informal letter endings

Love,
Lots of love,
All my love,
Best wishes,
All the best,

Unit 9

Verb + object + infinitive

Someone	advised	me	to do (something).
	allowed	you	
	encouraged	him	
	expected	her	
	forbade	us	
	forced	them	
	helped	Barbara	
	invited	the children	
	persuaded		
	preferred		
	reminded		
	told		
	wanted		

here/there + infinitive

I'm (not)	here	to	(do) that.
	there		listen.
			give an opinion.

too + adjective + infinitive

| He's | too | young | to (do) that. |
| | | tired | |

seem + infinitive

We seem to have fights all the time.

Unit 10

do and *make* (1)

Have you done your homework yet?
I'm doing the dishes.
I have to make my bed first.
Is Dad making dinner tonight?

Unit 11

Requests and inquiries

Lend me 50 cents.
Close the door, will you?
Do you need some help?
Would you turn down the radio, please?

Can I	ask you something?
Could I	
May I	
Do you mind if I	

I wonder if I could ask you something.
Would you mind doing something?
I wonder if you'd mind doing something.
Would you be kind enough to do something?
Would you be so kind as to do something?
I wonder if you can/could help me.

Responses

Not at all. There you go.
No, go right ahead.
I don't mind at all. Please do.
Thank you very much.
No, thanks. I'm just looking.
Of course.

Unit 12

Noun + infinitive

I have three more <u>shirts to pack</u>.
Do you have a <u>book to read</u> on the plane?
Which key? <u>The key to lock</u> the suitcase.

Pronoun/adverb + infinitive

There's <u>nothing to worry</u> about.
Is there <u>someone to meet</u> you in Los Angeles?
I asked <u>them to make</u> it.

Remember/Forget + infinitive

He remembered to pack his shirts.
He forgot to bring a book.

Unit 13

Verb + infinitive

expect	to do
remind	
would like	
hope	

Unit 16

Infinitives with and without *to*

| make/let | someone | do | something |
| force/allow | | to do | |

Unit 17

Stating preferences

I like this./I'd like to do that.
Which do you like better?
I like both.

I prefer this./I'd prefer to do that.
Which do you prefer?/Which would you prefer to do?
I don't like either one of them.

I'd rather do this./I'd rather not do this./I'd much rather do this.
Which would you rather do?
There isn't much choice.
I can't make up my mind.

Unit 18

Advisability and desirability (1) (*ought to, had better/better not*)

They ought to (do this)./They shouldn't (do that).
What should they do?

| We | 'd | better | do it. |
| | had | better not | |

Unit 20

Speculating about the present (1)

It's certainly… I'm almost certain…	It must be…
It's probably…	It could be… It may be…
It's possibly…	It might be…
It's probably not…	It can't be…
It's definitely not…	It couldn't be…

Unit 21

Speculating about the present (2)

They	must may might can't couldn't	be (doing that).

She's	probably	(doing that).

Have + noun

to have	a fight a party a good time a seat

Unit 22

Obligations, duties, preferences

She	should shouldn't	be doing that.
	ought to ought not to is supposed to isn't supposed to had better (not)	
	would rather would rather not	

Unit 23

do and *make* (2)

I kept doing the crossword.
I'd gone into New York to do some shopping.
I made plans.
She didn't want to make a scene.
She was making me (feel) so nervous.

Unit 25

Speculating about the past (1)

Could	it have been	him? her? them?

It	must could(n't) may (not) might (not)	have been	him. her.

(Unit 25 continued)

Could	he she they	have	done it? killed him? shot him?

He She They	must could may (not) might (not) can't couldn't	have	done it. killed him. shot him.

Unit 27

Advisability and desirability (2)

He	should shouldn't ought to ought not to	have done that.

Unit 28

Review: passives

| Someone did it. | It was done. |
| Someone did them. | They were done. |

| Someone had done it. | It had been done. |

| Someone was doing it. | It was being done. |
| Someone was doing them. | They were being done. |

Unit 29

Speculating about the past (2)

They	must should(n't) may (not) might (not) might even could(n't) can't	have been doing it.

Infinitive of purpose

The mother jumped in <u>to save</u> her.
They launched a lifeboat <u>to rescue</u> her.

Unit 31

Making and accepting apologies

I'm (terribly) sorry.
I really am sorry.
I wanted to apologize.
It won't happen again.
It wasn't my fault.
I didn't (see the sign).
I didn't realize.
I couldn't (find a parking space).
It was (so) dumb of me to….
What else can I say?

Don't worry about it.
Accidents happen.
Forget it.
It's nothing.

Unit 32

Verb + -ing/infinitive

stop	doing	stop	to do
remember		remember	
		forget	

Unit 34

Conditionals (type 1) with *unless*

If you do this, I'll do that.
If she doesn't do this, he'll do that.
Unless she does this, he'll do that.

Unit 35

Conditionals (type 2) with *unless*

If you did this, I'd do that.
If you didn't do this, I wouldn't do that.
Unless you did this, I wouldn't do that.

Unit 37

would have done

Would you have said anything?
What would you have done?

I	'd	have	said	something.
	would		done	anything.
	wouldn't			

Unit 38

Conditionals (type 3)

If	I	'd	done that,	I	'd	have	done this.
	he	had	seen that,	he	would	've	seen this.
	she	hadn't	been there,	she	wouldn't		known this.
	we	had not		we	would not		
	you			you			
	they			they			

Unit 40

Conditionals (type 3) with *unless* and *if only*

<u>Unless</u> you had studied film history, you would never have heard of most of them.
We wouldn't have gone on this trip <u>unless</u> it had been an escorted tour group.
<u>If only</u> (we'd had our grandchildren with us)!

Unit 42

Wishes (1)

I wish I	was there.
	wasn't here.
	was working there.
	wasn't working here.
	had	a car.
	didn't have	to do it.

(Unit 42 continued)

I wish I	could do it.	
	'd	done it.
	had	
	hadn't	
	worked	there.
	didn't work	here.

Unit 43

Expressing regret and opinions about the past

I wish they	had	done this.
	hadn't	

If I'd (done this),	(that) would have happened.
	I would be/know…

I'm sorry (it happened).	My only/biggest regret is…
I regret	it.	It's too bad that…
	(doing that).	

Unit 44

Wishes (2)

If you could	make	a wish,	what	would it be?
	have			would you wish for?

I'd wish for world peace/an end to famine.

Unit 45

Defining relative clauses

He	is the one	who	does	that.
She	's	that	did	
It		which		
She		that		
Those	are the ones	who	do	it.
They	're	which	did	
		that		

He's	the one. I saw	him.
She's		her.
It's		it.
They're	the ones. I saw	them.

He's	the one I saw.
She's	
It's	
They're	the ones I saw.

Unit 46

Defining relative clauses with *where* and *whose*

He went to California, where he did this.

He was looking for someone whose uniform he could steal.
A woman, whose hands were tied, was lying beside him.

Unit 48

Non-defining relative clauses with *who*, *which*, and *whose*

Alan Wolfe, who again escaped from the Maryland penitentiary, has been recaptured.

The construction industry, which is an important indicator of the economy's direction, reports fewer new buildings started in the last three months.

Tim Miles, the racing driver whose legs were badly injured in last year's Grand Prix accident, says he will never race again.

Central Motors' Calypso, whose success has surprised CM officials as much as the competition, is now the best-selling car in the United States.

Unit 49

Relative clauses in formal writing

to/for/from/on/in/about/through/of/with	which
	whom

Defining relative clauses in formal written style

He was the man to whom I spoke.

Defining relative clauses in spoken or informal style

He was the man	*I spoke to.*
	who I spoke to.
	that I spoke to.

Non-defining relative clauses in formal written style

Katherine Horton, <u>with whom you spoke,</u> is in charge of all conferences.

Non-defining relative clauses in spoken or informal style

Katherine Horton, <u>who you spoke to,</u> is in charge of all conferences.

Unit 53

Purpose clauses (1)
In order to...

In order to	*do that, we*	*need to*	*do this.*
To		*will*	
			did this.

or

We	*need to*	*do this,*	*in order to*	*do that.*
	will		*to*	
		did this		

For the purpose of

For the purpose of doing that, we (need to) do this.
We (need to) do this, for the purpose of doing that.

Unit 54

Purpose clauses (2)
so that

I did this so that	*he*	*could*	*do that.*
	she	*couldn't*	
	this	*would*	*happen.*
	that	*wouldn't*	

I'm doing this	*so that*	*he*	*can*	*do that.*
		she	*can't*	
		this	*will*	*happen.*
		that	*won't*	

or

So that	*he*	*could*	*do that,*	*I did this.*
	she	*couldn't*		
	this	*would*	*happen,*	
	that	*wouldn't*		

So that	*he*	*can't*	*do that,*	*I'm doing this.*
	she	*can*		
	this	*will*	*happen,*	*I do this.*
	that	*won't*		

Unit 55

Purpose clauses (3)—negatives

Do this	*so that you don't*	*do that.*
	in order not to	

Do this	*to*	*avoid*	*that.*
	in order to		*doing that.*
	so that you can		

Do this	*to prevent*	*that (from happening).*
	to stop	*something (from) happening.*
	to keep	*somebody (from) doing that.*

Unit 56

Result clauses
so ... (that)

The house was so beautiful (that) they bought it.

She had so	*much work*	*(that) she couldn't sleep.*
	many problems	

They worked so much (that) they hardly ever saw each other.

such ... (that)

It was such a beautiful house (that) they bought it.

She had such a lot of	*work*	*(that) she couldn't sleep.*
	problems	

They worked such long hours (that) they hardly ever saw each other.

Unit 58

Clauses of reason and contrast (1)
because

It was raining. She took her umbrella.
She took her umbrella because it was raining.

although, though, even though

It wasn't raining. He took his umbrella.

He took his umbrella	*although* *though* *even though*	*it wasn't raining.*

Unit 60

Clauses of reason and contrast (2)
because/due to/although/in spite of/despite/
however/nevertheless

It was snowing, so they canceled the game.

or

They canceled the game	*because it was snowing.* *because of | the snow.* *due to*

or

Because it was snowing, *Because of | the snow* *Due to*	*they canceled the game.*

(continued)

(Unit 60 continued)

It was snowing, but they didn't cancel the game.

or

They didn't cancel the game	*although it was snowing.* *in spite of | the snow.* *despite*

or

Although it was snowing, *In spite of | the snow,* *Despite*	*they didn't cancel the game.*

It was hard, but she managed to win.

or

It was hard.	*However,* *Nevertheless,*	*she managed to win.*

or

It was hard.	*She managed to win,*	*however.* *nevertheless.*

or

It was hard. She managed,	*however,* *nevertheless,*	*to win.*

Unit 62

Structures with *what* as object or subject

I don't know what to do with him.
That's not what we're here for.
What I saw surprised me.

Unit 63

whatever, whichever, whoever, whenever, wherever, however

What should I do?	*I don't mind.*	*Do whatever you like.*	*Whatever you want to.*
Which one can I take?	*It doesn't matter.*	*Take whichever one you like.*	*Whichever you like.*
Who should I ask?	*I don't know.*	*Ask whoever is there.*	*Whoever is there.*
When can I do it?	*I don't care.*	*Do it whenever you like.*	*Whenever you like.*
Where should I go?	*I'm not sure.*	*Go wherever you want to.*	*Wherever you want.*
How should I do it?	*It isn't important.*	*Do it however you like.*	*However you like.*

Unit 67

Expressions with *rather*

I'd rather | *go there.*

| *I'd rather* | *you, he, she* | *went there.* |
| | *we, they* | *didn't go there.* |

Expressions with *time*

It's (about) time	*to go.*
	we left.
	we were leaving.

as if/though

| *It isn't as* | *if* | *this were my first visit.* |
| | *though* | *he didn't know.* |

Unit 69

Review: passives (1)

It	*is*	*done.*
	was	
	has been	
They	*are*	
	were	
	are being	
	have been	

It	*will*	*be done.*
	can	
	may	
	might	
	has to	
	should	

Unit 70

Review: passives (2)

It	*is*	*being done.*
	was	
They	*are*	
	were	

| *It* | *had been* | *done.* |
| *They* | | |

Unit 71

Extension of passives

| *There's a lot <u>to be done</u>* | *before the circus arrives.* |
| *It <u>will have been done</u>* | *by 7:30.* |

Unit 72

to have/get something done

I'm having	*the car tuned up.*
I have to get	*my hair done.*
	the house painted.
	the ceiling fixed.

(Unit 72 continued)

needs to be done

| *The* | *floor* | *needs to be* | *swept.* |
| | *house* | | *painted.* |

needs doing

| *The* | *floor* | *needs* | *sweeping.* |
| | *house* | | *painting.* |

Unit 74

verb + object + infinitive

Tell	*me*	*to do something.*
Ask	*them*	*not to do something.*
Remind	*someone*	
Invite	*us*	
Advise	*her*	
Promise	*him*	
Warn		
Order		
Instruct		
Force		
Beg		

Unit 75

Reported speech (2)

am/is	→	*was*	*"It's important."* *She said that it was important.*
are	→	*were*	*"They're going to be late."* *She said (that) they were going to be late.*
have/has	→	*had*	*"I've done the letters."* *She said (that) she had done the letters.*
don't	→	*didn't*	*"I don't know."* *She said (that) she didn't know.*
want	→	*wanted*	*"I want a day off."* *She said (that) she wanted a day off.*
didn't do	→	*hadn't done*	*"I didn't finish it."* *She said (that) she hadn't finished it.*
saw	→	*had seen*	*"I saw him."* *She said (that) she had seen him.*
was/were	→	*had been*	*"I wasn't there."* *She said (that) she hadn't been there.*
will/won't	→	*would/wouldn't*	*"I won't do it."* *She said (that) she wouldn't do it.*
can/can't	→	*could/couldn't*	*"I can't do it."* *She said (that) she couldn't do it.*

(Unit 75 continued)

may	→	might	*"I may do it."* *She said (that) she* *might do it.*
had done	→	no change	*"I had done it."* *She said (that) she had* *done it.*
would			
could			
should			
ought			
might			

Other words that may change:

this	→	that
these	→	those
here	→	there
now	→	then
yesterday	→	the day before
tomorrow	→	the next day
this (week)	→	that (week)
last (month)	→	the (month) before
next (year)	→	the next (year)

Unit 76

Reported speech (3)

"What was the immediate effect of this peace agreement?"
She asked what the immediate effect of that peace agreement had been.

"The first thing was an immediate cease-fire."
He said that the first thing had been an immediate cease-fire.

"Have both parties honored the cease-fire?"
She asked if both parties had honored the cease-fire.

"Oh, yes. So far."
He said that both parties had so far.